MARIJUANA NATION

THE LEGALIZATION OF CANNABIS ACROSS THE USA

By The Associated Press

Mango Media
Miami
in collaboration with
The Associated Press

  AP EDITIONS

AP Editions

Copyright © 2015 Associated Press. All rights reserved. This material may not be published, broadcast, rewritten or redistributed.

Published by Mango Media, Inc.
www.mangomedia.us

No part of this publication may be reproduced, distributed or transmitted in any form or by any means, without prior written permission.

This is a work of non-fiction adapted from articles and content by journalists of The Associated Press and published with permission.

Marijuana Nation *The Legalization of Cannabis Across the USA*
ISBN: 978-1-63353-036-2

Cover Photo:

A caregiver picks out a marijuana bud for a patient at a marijuana dispensary in Denver. On May 7, 2014, Colorado lawmakers approved an uninsured coop banking scheme, another step to institutionalize the cash-only marijuana industry, September 18, 2012. (AP Photo/Ed Andrieski, File)

Publisher's Note

AP Editions brings together stories and photographs by the professional journalists of The Associated Press.

These stories are presented in their original form and are intended to provide a snapshot of history as the moments occurred.

We hope you enjoy these selections from the front lines of newsgathering.

"No one knows, when he places a marijuana cigarette to his lips, whether he will become a philosopher, a joyous reveler in a musical heaven, a mad insensate, a calm philosopher, or a murderer."

- Harry Anslinger,
Former Commissioner of the Bureau of Prohibition, 1937

Table of Contents

- Overview 1
- A History of Marijuana 3
- The Road: Colorado And Washington 13
- Economics 27
- Regulations 39
- The Stoner Stereotype.. 53
- The Perception of Marijuana Across the Country 65
- At the Ballot Box... 75
- The NFL 79
- The Future 89
- Business Savvy 99
- Avoiding the Issue for Too Long 107
- Marijuana Visualized 123

Overview

The use of recreational marijuana is legal in Colorado and Washington. Alaska, Oregon and Washington, D.C., might soon follow their example. Yet, federal law continues to label all use of marijuana as an illegal act.

In Rhode Island and Vermont, proposals to have marijuana legalized recreationally in 2015 have been placed on the ballot. Similarly, Arizona, California, Maine, Massachusetts and Nevada are each expected to address the issue in the coming year.

Could your state be next?

In *Marijuana Nation*, the journalists and photographers of The Associated Press follow the shifting U.S climate on legalizing marijuana and chart its cultural and legal implications. They also cover the debates spawned by this growing movement, which has many supporters believing it's "high" time for America to embrace the legal use of marijuana once and for all.

1

A History of Marijuana

From the Revolution to Today
December 6, 2012
By Gene Johnson

One-to-two-week-old marijuana starts sit under lights at a growing facility in Seattle, April 4, 2013. (AP Photo/Elaine Thompson)

The grass is no greener. But, finally, it's legal — at least somewhere in America. It's been a long, strange trip for marijuana.

Washington state and Colorado voted to legalize and regulate its recreational use in November of 2012. But before that, the plant, renowned since ancient times for its strong fibers, medical use and mind-altering properties, was a staple crop of the colonies, an "assassin of youth," a counterculture emblem and a widely accepted — if often abused — medicine.

On the occasion of "Legalization Day," when Washington's new law took effect, here's a look back at the cultural and legal status of the "evil weed" in American history.

George Washington and Thomas Jefferson both grew hemp and puzzled over the best ways to process it for clothing and rope.

Indeed, cannabis has been grown in America since soon after the British arrived. In 1619 the Crown ordered the colonists at Jamestown to grow hemp to satisfy England's incessant demand for maritime ropes, Wayne State University professor Ernest Abel wrote in "Marihuana: The First Twelve Thousand Years."

This file photo shows former President Thomas Jefferson's home, Monticello, in Charlottesville, Va. Jefferson and George Washington both grew hemp and puzzled over the best ways to process it for clothing and rope. Indeed, cannabis has been grown in America since soon after the British arrived, April 22, 2009. (AP Photo/Steve Helber, File)

Hemp became more important to the colonies as New England's own shipping industry developed, and homespun hemp helped clothe American soldiers during the Revolutionary War. Some colonies offered farmers "bounties" for growing it.

"We have manufactured within our families the most necessary articles of clothing," Jefferson said in "Notes on the State of Virginia." "Those of wool, flax and hemp are very coarse, unsightly, and unpleasant."

Jefferson went on to invent a device for processing hemp in 1815.

TASTE THE HASHISH

Books such as "The Arabian Nights" and Alexandre Dumas' "The Count of Monte Cristo," with its voluptuous descriptions of hashish highs in the exotic Orient, helped spark a cannabis fad among intellectuals in the mid-19th century.

"But what changes occur!" one of Dumas' characters tells an uninitiated acquaintance. "When you return to this mundane sphere from your visionary world, you would seem to leave a Neapolitan spring for a Lapland winter -- to quit paradise for earth -- heaven for hell!

Taste the hashish, guest of mine -- taste the hashish. After the Civil War, with hospitals often overprescribing opiates for pain, many soldiers returned home hooked on harder drugs.

Those addictions eventually became a public health concern. In 1906, Congress passed the Pure Food and Drug Act, requiring labeling of ingredients, and states began regulating opiates and other medicines — including cannabis.

Narcotics Commissioner Harry J. Anslinger announces a series of raids in the nation's big cities aimed at crippling the narcotics traffic in New York. More than 500 suspected peddlers were bagged, January 4, 1958. (AP Photo)

MEXICAN FOLKLORE AND JAZZ CLUBS

By the turn of the 20th century, cannabis smoking remained little known in the United States — but that was changing, thanks largely to The Associated Press, says Isaac Campos, a Latin American history professor at the University of Cincinnati.

"But what changes occur!" one of Dumas' characters tells an uninitiated acquaintance. "When you return to this mundane sphere from your visionary world, you would seem to leave a Neapolitan spring for a Lapland winter -- to quit paradise for earth -- heaven for hell! Taste the hashish, guest of mine -- taste the hashish. After the Civil War, with hospitals often overprescribing opiates for pain, many soldiers returned home hooked on harder drugs.

This undated file photo provided by the Drug Enforcement Administration shows a 1930s anti-marijuana movie poster as part of an exhibit at the DEA Museum and Visitors Center which opened in Arlington, Va., May 10, 1999. (AP Photo/DEA, File)

Those addictions eventually became a public health concern. In 1906, Congress passed the Pure Food and Drug Act, requiring labeling of ingredients, and states began regulating opiates and other medicines — including cannabis.

In the 1890s, the first English-language newspaper opened in Mexico and, through the wire service, tales of marijuana-induced violence that were common in Mexican papers began to appear north of the border — helping to shape public perceptions that would later form the basis of pot prohibition, Campos says.

By 1910, when the Mexican Revolution pushed immigrants north, articles in the New York Sun, Boston Daily Globe and other papers decried the "evils of ganjah smoking" and suggested that some use it "to key themselves up to the point of killing."

This file image made from a film produced by the U.S. Department of Agriculture during World War II shows the title frame of the movie "Hemp for Victory." After Japanese troops cut off access to Asian fiber supplies during the war, it released the propaganda film urging farmers to grow hemp and extolling its use in parachutes and rope for the war effort. (AP Photo/U.S. Department of Agriculture, File)

Pot-smoking spread through the 1920s and became especially popular with jazz musicians. Louis Armstrong, a lifelong fan and defender of the drug he called "gage," was arrested in California in 1930 and given a six-month suspended sentence for pot possession.

"It relaxes you, makes you forget all the bad things that happen to a Negro," he once said. In the 1950s, he urged legalization in a letter to President Dwight Eisenhower.

REEFER MADNESS, HEMP FOR VICTORY

After the repeal of alcohol prohibition in 1933, Harry Anslinger, who headed the federal Bureau of Narcotics, turned his attention to pot. He told of sensational crimes reportedly committed by marijuana addicts. "No one knows, when he places a marijuana cigarette to his lips, whether he will become a philosopher, a joyous reveler in a musical heaven, a mad insensate, a calm philosopher, or a murderer," he wrote in a 1937 magazine article called "Marijuana: Assassin of Youth." The hysteria was captured in the propaganda films of the time — most famously, "Reefer Madness," which depicted young adults descending into violence and insanity after smoking marijuana.

Music fans seek shelter is a grass hut at the Woodstock Music and Art Festival in Bethel, New York. Sign above reads "Have a Marijuana," August 17, 1969. (AP Photo)

The movie found little audience upon its release in 1936 but was rediscovered by pot fans in the 1970s. Congress banned marijuana with the Marihuana Tax Act of 1937. Anslinger continued his campaign into the '40s and '50s, sometimes trying — without luck — to get jazz musicians to inform on each other. "Zoot suited hep cats, with their jive lingo and passion for swift, hot music, provide a fertile field for growth of the marijuana habit, narcotics agents have found here," began a 1943 Washington Post story about increasing pot use in the nation's capital. The Department of Agriculture promoted a different message. After Japanese troops cut off access to

Asian fiber supplies during World War II, it released "Hemp For Victory," a propaganda film urging farmers to grow hemp and extolling its use in parachutes and rope for the war effort.

COUNTERCULTURE

As the conformity of the postwar era took hold, getting high on marijuana and other drugs emerged as a symbol of the counterculture, with Jack Kerouac and the rest of the Beat Generation singing pot's praises. It also continued to be popular with actors and musicians. When actor Robert Mitchum was arrested on a marijuana charge in 1948, People magazine recounted, "The press nationwide branded him a dope fiend. Preachers railed against him from pulpits. Mothers warned their daughters to shun his films." Congress responded to increasing drug use — especially heroin — with stiffer penalties in the '50s.

Anslinger began to hype what we now call the "gateway drug" theory: that marijuana had to be controlled because it would eventually lead its users to heroin. Then came Vietnam. The widespread, open use of marijuana by hippies and war protesters from San Francisco to Woodstock finally exposed the falsity of the claims so many had made about marijuana leading to violence, says University of Virginia professor Richard Bonnie, a scholar of pot's cultural status. In 1972, Bonnie was the associate director of a commission appointed by President Richard Nixon to study marijuana. The commission said marijuana should be decriminalized and regulated. Nixon rejected that, but a dozen states in the '70s went on to eliminate jail time as a punishment for pot arrests.

"JUST SAY NO"

The push to liberalize drug laws hit a wall by the late 1970s. Parents groups became concerned about data showing that more children were using drugs, and at a younger age. The religious right was emerging as a force in national politics. And the first "Cheech and Chong" movie, in 1978, didn't do much to burnish pot's image. When she became first lady, Nancy Reagan quickly promoted the anti-drug cause. During a visit with schoolchildren in Oakland, Calif., as Reagan later recalled, "A little girl raised her hand and said, 'Mrs. Reagan, what do you do if somebody offers you drugs?' And I said, 'Well, you just say no.' And there it was born." By 1988, more than 12,000 "Just Say No" clubs and school programs had been formed, according to the Ronald Reagan Presidential Foundation and Library. Between 1978 and 1987, the percentage of high school seniors reporting daily use of marijuana fell from 10 percent to 3 percent. And marijuana use was so politically toxic that when Bill Clinton ran for president in 1992, he said he "didn't inhale."

First lady Nancy Reagan sits with a fourth and fifth grade class at Island Park Elementary School on Mercer Island, Wash. where she participated in a drug education class. At left is Amy Clarfeld, 10, and Andrew Cary, 10, is at right. During a visit with schoolchildren in Oakland, Calif., Reagan later recalled, "A little girl raised her hand and said, 'Mrs. Reagan, what do you do if somebody offers you drugs?' And I said, 'Well, you just say no.' And there it was born," February 14, 1984. (AP Photo/Barry Sweet, File)

MEDS OF A DIFFERENT SORT

People attending an Amendment 64 watch party celebrate after a local television station announced the marijuana amendment's passage in Denver, Colo., November 6, 2012. (AP Photo/Brennan Linsley)

Marijuana has been used as medicine since ancient times, as described in Chinese, Indian and Roman texts, but U.S. drug laws in the latter part of the 20th century made no room for it. In the 1970s, many states passed symbolic laws calling for studies of marijuana's efficacy as medicine, although virtually no studies ever took place because of the federal prohibition. Nevertheless, doctors noted its ability to ease nausea and stimulate appetites of cancer and AIDS patients. And in 1996, California became the first state to allow the medical use of marijuana. Since then, 17 other states and the District of Columbia have followed.

In recent years, medical marijuana dispensaries — readily identifiable by the green crosses on their storefronts — have proliferated in many states, including Washington, Colorado and California. That's prompted a backlash from some who suggest they are fronts for illicit drug dealing and that most of the people they serve aren't really sick. The Justice Department has shut down some it deems the worst offenders.

LEGAL WEED AT LAST

On Nov. 6, of 2012 Washington and Colorado pleased aging hippies everywhere — and shocked straights of all ages — by voting to become the first states to legalize the fun use of marijuana. Voters handily approved measures to decriminalize the possession of up to an ounce by adults over 21. Colorado's measure also permits home-growing of up to six plants. Both states are working to set up a regulatory scheme with licensed growers, processors and retail stores. Eventually, activists say, grown-ups will be able to walk into a store, buy some marijuana, and walk out with ganja in hand — but not before paying the taxman. The states expect to raise hundreds of millions of dollars for schools and other government functions. But it's not so simple. The regulatory schemes conflict with the federal government's longstanding pot prohibition, according to many legal scholars. The Justice Department could sue to block those schemes from taking effect — but hasn't said whether it will do so. The bizarre journey of cannabis in America continues.

The Road: Colorado And Washington

Marijuana as Medicine
November 7, 2012
By Kristen Wyatt

This file photo shows a medical marijuana plant at a dispensary in Seattle, November 7, 2012. (AP Photo/Ted S. Warren, File)

Now comes legal pot for the people. Those who have argued for decades that legalizing and taxing weed would be better than a costly, failed U.S. drug war have their chance to prove it, as Colorado and Washington became the first states to allow pot for recreational use.

While the measures earned support from broad swaths of the electorate in both states Tuesday, November 7, 2012 they are likely to face resistance from federal drug warriors. As of Wednesday, the 8th authorities did not say whether they would challenge the new laws. Pot advocates say a fight is exactly what they want. "I think we are at a tipping point on marijuana policy," said Brian Vicente, co-author of Colorado's marijuana measure. "We are going to see whether marijuana prohibition survives, or whether we should try a new and more sensible approach." Soon after the measures passed, cheering people poured out of bars in Denver, the tangy scent of pot filling the air, and others in Seattle lit up in celebration.

Authorities in Colorado, however, urged caution. "Federal law still says marijuana is an illegal drug, so don't break out the Cheetos or Goldfish too quickly," said Democratic Gov. John Hickenlooper, who opposed the measure. As the initial celebration dies down and the process to implement the laws progresses over the next year, other states and countries will be watching to see if the measures can both help reduce money going to drug cartels and raise it for governments.

Governments in Latin America where drugs are produced for the U.S. market were largely quiet about the measures, but the main adviser to Mexico's president-elect said the new laws will force the U.S. and his country to reassess how they fight cross-border pot smuggling. Analysts said that there would likely be an impact on cartels in Mexico that send pot to the U.S., but differed on how soon and how much. Both measures call for the drug to be heavily taxed, with the profits headed to state coffers.

Colorado would devote the potential tax revenue first to school construction, while Washington's sends pot taxes to an array of health programs. Estimates vary widely on how much they would raise. Colorado officials anticipate somewhere between $5 million and $22 million a year. Washington analysts estimated legal pot could produce nearly $2 billion over five years. Both state estimates came with big caveats: The current illegal marijuana market is hard to gauge and any revenue would be contingent upon federal authorities allowing commercial pot sales in the first place, something that is very much still in question. Both measures remove criminal penalties for adults over 21 possessing small amounts of the drug — the boldest rejection of pot prohibition laws passed across the country in the 1930s. Pot has come a long way since. In the 1960s, it was a counterculture fixture. In 1971, President Richard Nixon declared the War on Drugs. Twenty-five years later, California approved medical marijuana.

Now, 17 states and Washington, D.C., allow it. Meanwhile, many more cities either took pot possession crimes off the books or directed officers to make marijuana arrests a low priority. On Tuesday night, broad sections of the electorate in Colorado and Washington backed the measures, some because they thought the drug war had failed and others because they viewed potential revenue as a boon for their states in lean times. A similar measure in Oregon failed. "People think little old ladies with glaucoma should be able to use marijuana. This is different. This is a step further than anything we have seen to date," said Sam Kamin, a University of Denver law professor who has studied the history of pot prohibition. The Justice Department says it is evaluating the measures. When California was considering legalization in 2010,

This photo shows a one-gram packet of a variety of recreational marijuana named "Space Needle" during packaging operations at Sea of Green Farms in Seattle. Each packet is labeled with the percentage of THC, a lot number, and warning messages, July 1, 2014. (AP Photo/Ted S. Warren)

Attorney General Eric Holder said it would be a "significant impediment" to joint federal and local efforts to combat drug traffickers. Federal agents have cracked down on medical pot dispensaries in states where it is legal, including California and Washington. Individual pot users may not be immediately impacted, as authorities have long focused on dismantling trafficking operations. Peter Bensinger, administrator of the Drug Enforcement Administration from 1976 to 1981, and other former DEA heads urged Holder to make more noise this year about the pot votes. Colorado was a critical state for President Barack Obama's re-election. Now, he said, "I can't see the Justice Department doing anything other than enforce the law. There's no other out."

Brian Smith of the Washington State Liquor Control Board, which will implement the new law, said officials are waiting anxiously to find out what federal law enforcement authorities plan to do. "They have been silent," Smith said. Both states will have about a year to come up with rules for their legal pot systems. In Mexico, which produces much of the pot that gets into the U.S. and where cartels and the government are embroiled in a yearslong deadly battle, the man in charge of Enrique Pena Nieto's presidential transition said the administration opposed legalization. "These important modifications change somewhat the rules of the games in the relationship with the United States," Luis Videgaray told Radio Formula.

A customer pays cash for retail marijuana at 3D Cannabis Center in Denver. Frustrated by the cash-heavy aspect of its new marijuana industry, Colorado is trying a long-shot bid to create a financial system devoted to the pot business, May 8, 2014. (AP Photo/Brennan Linsley)

A former high-ranking official in the country's internal intelligence service who has studied the potential effects of legalization said he was optimistic that the measures would damage the cartels, possibly cutting profits from $6 billion to $4.6 billion. Alejandro Hope, now an analyst at the think tank Mexican Competitiveness Institute, said among the complicating factors could be whether a strong U.S. crackdown on legal pot could negate all but the smallest effects on the cartels.

In Seattle, John Davis, a medical marijuana provider, called passage of the state's measure "a significant movement in the right direction." But he said he expected some confrontation with federal authorities. "This law does not prevent conflicts," he said, adding that its passage "will highlight the necessity to find some kind of resolution between state and federal laws."

Colorado Marijuana Regulations Signed into Law
May 28, 2013
By Kristen Wyatt

A set of laws to govern how recreational marijuana should be grown, sold and taxed was signed into law on Tuesday, May 28, 2013 in Colorado, where

Democratic Gov. John Hickenlooper called the measures the state's best attempt to navigate the uncharted territory of legalized recreational pot.

The laws cover how the drug should be raised and packaged, with purchasing limits for out-of-state visitors and a new marijuana driving limit as an analogy to blood alcohol levels. Hickenlooper didn't support marijuana legalization last year, but he praised the regulatory package as a good first crack at safely overseeing the drug. "Recreational marijuana is really a completely new entity," Hickenlooper said, calling the pot rules "commonsense" oversight, such as required potency labeling and a requirement that marijuana is to be sold in child-proof opaque packing with labels clearly stating the drug may not be safe.

Colorado voters approved recreational marijuana as a constitutional amendment last year. The state allows adults over 21 to possess up to an ounce of the drug. Adults can grow up to six plants, or buy pot in retail stores, which are slated to open in January.

The governor said Tuesday he believes the federal government will soon respond to the fact that Colorado and Washington state are in violation of federal drug law. But Hickenlooper didn't have a specific idea of when. "We think that it will be relatively soon. We are optimistic that they are going to be a little more specific in their approach on this issue," Hickenlooper said.

Pressed for details, the governor jokingly referred to unrelated scandals surrounding the U.S. Department of Justice. "They've been kind of busy," Hickenlooper said. Colorado's new marijuana laws include buying limits for out-of-state visitors. Visitors over 21 would be limited to one-fourth of an ounce in a single retail transaction, though they could legally possess the full ounce.

Colorado laws attempt to curb public use of marijuana by banning its sale in places that sell food and drink that aren't infused with the drug, an attempt to prevent Amsterdam-style pot cafes. Food laced with the drug also would have to be to-go orders. Colorado's laws also include a first-in-the-nation requirement that marijuana magazines such as High Times be kept behind the counter in stores that allow people under 21.

That provision has prompted promises by attorneys representing at least two publications to challenge the restriction, which would treat pot magazines similar to pornography. Besides the magazine restriction, Colorado's laws differ in several more ways from proposed marijuana regulations pending in Washington state. Colorado makes no attempt to ban concentrated marijuana, or hashish, unlike Washington. Colorado also has different possession limits on edible marijuana.

Colorado also is planning a brief grandfather period during which only current medical marijuana business owners could sell recreational pot. Both states are poised to require all pot-related businesses to have security systems, 24-hour video surveillance and insurance. One of the Colorado laws signed Tuesday gives state pot businesses a chance to claim business deductions on their taxes, something currently prohibited because the industry is illegal under federal law.

Lewis Koski, left, chief investigator of the Colorado Marijuana Enforcement Division, demonstrates a handheld radio-frequency reader, which is part of its new marijuana inventory tracking system, known as MITS, during a news conference, in Denver, Wednesday, Dec. 11, 2013. (AP Photo/Brennan Linsley)

Colorado's laws also propose a series of new taxes on the drug. If voters agree this fall, recreational pot would face a 15 percent excise tax, with the proceeds marked for school construction.

There would also be a new recreational pot sales tax of 10 percent, in addition to regular statewide and local sales taxes. The special sales tax would be spent on marijuana regulation and new educational efforts to keep the drug away from children. "Public safety and the safety of our children were at the forefront of our minds," said Sen. Randy Baumgardner, R-Hot Sulphur Springs, the sponsor of some of the pot bills.

Lawmakers and a few dozen marijuana legalization activists on hand to see the pot bills signed into law agreed that marijuana laws will see many changes in coming years if the federal government doesn't intervene. "We are going to be talking about marijuana in the state of Colorado for some time," predicted Rep. Mark Waller, R-Colorado Springs, a sponsor of the stoned-driving law.

Mason Tvert, spokesman for the national legalization advocacy group the Marijuana Policy Project, predicted a lot of states will watch to see how recreational pot regulation works in Colorado and Washington. "We can regulate the sale of alcohol in a responsible manner, and there's no reason we can't regulate the sale of something objectively less harmful — marijuana," Tvert said.

Eggs are added into a mixer with green cannabis-infused "canna butter" in a stainless steel bowl at the start of batter mixing for peanut butter jelly cups, inside Sweet Grass Kitchen, a well-established gourmet marijuana edibles bakery which sells its confections to retail outlets, in Denver, June 19, 2014. (AP Photo/Brennan Linsley)

US Drug War
October 12, 2013
By Kristen Wyatt

The federal government has reluctantly agreed to let Colorado be the first state to collect taxes from the legal sale of recreational marijuana, but it also has made clear it doesn't agree with the move and may try to stop it, if isn't tightly controlled. Instead of keeping a low profile with the money, however, some Colorado lawmakers are trying the bold move of using millions of dollars they've collected so far from pot sales to seek matching funds from the federal government to keep kids off drugs. The plan calls for transferring $3.5 million from the state's marijuana cash fund to its general fund and then sending the same amount to a state department that would apply for a federal match. Democratic state Sen. Pat Steadman, the measure's sponsor, joked that the bookkeeping move "is what I'm calling money laundering."

Supporters say the transfer shouldn't raise any concerns since federal authorities already collect marijuana dollars from the state's medical pot industry and have established guidelines for recreational sales that include keeping the drug away from minors and off federal lands.

Moving the money from one fund to another, proponents say, simply acknowledges and avoids potential conflict. Colorado just needs to do "a little two-step" to calm federal nerves, Steadman said, explaining the plan to fellow budget writers. "We wouldn't want the tainted money to draw a federal match, now, would we?" he added, sarcastically. Skeptics are rolling their eyes. "Colorado is now becoming basically a cartel, a drug cartel," said Sen. Kent Lambert, a Republican on the budget-writing committee, who nonetheless voted in favor. "I don't know what they're trying to do," Lambert said.

Maybe "avoid federal scrutiny? I don't think you're going to hide it from the federal government." The match request would seek funds from the U.S. Centers for Medicare & Medicaid Services "for behavioral health community programs for school-based prevention" of child drug use. Federal Medicaid authorities would have to approve the idea, but it's not immediately clear how the agency would respond. A CMS spokeswoman declined comment on Thursday, April 24th, 2014.

The idea of sending marijuana revenue to the state's general fund isn't new. Colorado has for years put a 2.9 percent sales tax on medical pot, with the revenue going to the general fund, which routinely sends money along to federal accounts. But the recreational sales industry has created enough cash that lawmakers for the first time will be able to seek a dollar-for-dollar match of pot money with federal money. In Washington state, where retail sales haven't yet begun, voters assigned a new dedicated marijuana fund to receive pot taxes and spend the money on health care, drug abuse treatment and education, and marijuana-related research. It's too soon to say whether Washington lawmakers would seek federal matching funds for any of those efforts in the future.

A spokesman for the Colorado department that would seek Medicaid funding insisted that the request to federal authorities will be from general fund dollars. "None of our programs seek funding from marijuana revenues," Marc Williams said in an email. Williams added that the prevention grants "would likely give preference to those programs operating in school districts or areas where there are a larger number of young, Medicaid-eligible clients." Steadman predicted the federal government would agree to the match. "As long as it is an eligible benefit within the Medicaid program and we're investing state dollars to expand benefits or expand the scope of our program, that's eligible for a federal match," Steadman said this week. "And apparently we should be doing that with general fund dollars, not marijuana tax fund dollars, although in my estimation, all of those dollars are the same shade of green," he said.

The U.S. Department of Justice said in a memo to the states last August that in order to avoid a crackdown on pot laws that flout the federal ban, certain conditions must be met. At the top of the list was keeping marijuana away from minors. Colorado legalized marijuana for all adults over 21 in 2012, though tax collections didn't start perking up until January, when retail sales began. Projections vary, but legislative budget-writers have projected marijuana taxes and fees will bring Colorado at least $67 million for the fiscal year that begins in July. The budget proposal, which includes a total of $31.4 million in marijuana spending, now faces debate from the full Legislature. Republican Rep. Cheri Gerou predicted a fight. "We're going to be picked apart, once this thing becomes public," she said.

INDUSTRIAL HEMP

Southeast Colorado farmer Ryan Loflin tried an illegal crop in 2013. He didn't hide it from neighbors, and he never feared law enforcement would come asking about it. Loflin is among about two dozen Colorado farmers who raised industrial hemp, marijuana's non-intoxicating cousin that can't be grown under federal drug law, and bringing in the nation's first acknowledged crop in more than five decades.

Emboldened by voters in Colorado and Washington in 2012 giving the green light to both marijuana and industrial hemp production, Loflin planted 55 acres of several varieties of hemp alongside his typical alfalfa and wheat crops.

The hemp came in sparse and scraggly this month, but Loflin said but he's still turning away buyers. "Phone's been ringing off the hook," said Loflin, who plans to press the seeds into oil and sell the fibrous remainder to buyers who'll use it in building materials, fabric and rope. "People want to buy more than I can grow." But hemp's economic prospects are far from certain. Finished hemp is legal in the U.S., but growing it remains off-limits under federal law. The Congressional Research Service recently noted wildly differing projections about hemp's economic potential. However, America is one of hemp's fastest-growing markets, with imports largely coming from China and Canada.

In 2011, the U.S. imported $11.5 million worth of hemp products, up from $1.4 million in 2000. Most of that is hemp seed and hemp oil, which finds its way into granola bars, soaps, lotions and even cooking oil. Whole Foods Market now sells hemp milk, hemp tortilla chips and hemp seeds coated in dark chocolate.

Colorado won't start granting hemp-cultivation licenses until 2014, but Loflin didn't wait. His confidence got a boost in August when the U.S. Department of Justice said the federal government would generally defer to state marijuana laws as long as states keep marijuana away from children and drug cartels. The memo didn't even mention hemp as an enforcement priority for the Drug Enforcement Administration.

"I figured they have more important things to worry about than, you know, rope," a smiling Loflin said as he hand-harvested 4-foot-tall plants on his Baca County land. Colorado's hemp experiment may not be unique for long. Ten states now have industrial hemp laws that conflict with federal drug policy, including one signed by California Gov. Jerry Brown last month. And it's not just the typical marijuana-friendly suspects: Kentucky, North Dakota and West Virginia have industrial hemp laws on the books. Hemp production was never banned outright, but it dropped to zero in the late 1950s because of competition from synthetic fibers and increasing anti-drug sentiment. Hemp and marijuana are the same species, Cannabis sativa, just cultivated differently to enhance or reduce marijuana's psychoactive chemical, THC.

The 1970 Controlled Substances Act required hemp growers to get a permit from the DEA, the last of which was issued in 1999 for a quarter-acre experimental plot in Hawaii. That permit expired in 2003. The U.S. Department of Agriculture last recorded an industrial hemp crop in the late 1950s, down from a 1943 peak of more than 150 million pounds on 146,200 harvested acres.

But Loflin and other legalization advocates say hemp is back in style and that federal obstacles need to go. Loflin didn't even have to hire help to bring in his crop, instead posting on Facebook that he needed volunteer harvesters. More than two dozen people showed up — from as far as Texas and Idaho. Volunteers pulled the plants up from the root and piled them whole on two flatbed trucks.

The mood was celebratory, people whooping at the sight of it and joking they thought they'd never see the day. But there are reasons to doubt hemp's viability. Even if law enforcement doesn't interfere, the market might. "It is not possible," Congressional Research Service researchers wrote in a July report, "to predict the potential market and employment effects of relaxing current restrictions on U.S. hemp production."

The most recent federal study came 13 years ago, when the USDA concluded the nation's hemp markets "are, and will likely remain, small" and "thin." And a 2004 study by the University of Wisconsin warned hemp "is not likely to generate sizeable profits" and highlighted "uncertainty about long-run demand for hemp products."

Still, there are seeds of hope. Global hemp production has increased from 250 million pounds in 1999 to more than 380 million pounds in 2011, according to United Nations agricultural surveys, which attributed the boost to increased demand for hemp seeds and hemp oil. Congress is paying attention to the country's increasing acceptance of hemp. The House version of the stalled farm bill includes an amendment, sponsored by lawmakers in Colorado, Oregon and Kentucky, allowing industrial hemp cultivation nationwide.

The amendment's prospects, like the farm bill's timely passage, are far from certain. Ron Carleton, a Colorado deputy agricultural commissioner who is heading up the state's looming hemp licensure, said he has no idea what hemp's commercial potential is. He's not even sure how many farmers will sign up for Colorado's licensure program next year, though he's fielded a "fair number of inquiries." "What's going to happen, we'll just have to see," Carleton said.

Poison Control?
January 23, 2015
By Gene Johnson

Marijuana-related calls to poison control centers in Washington and Colorado have spiked since the states began allowing legal sales last year, with an especially troubling increase in calls concerning young children.

But it's not clear how much of the increase might be related to more people using marijuana, as opposed to people feeling more comfortable to report their problems now that the drug is legal for adults over 21.

New year-end data being presented to Colorado's Legislature next week show that the Rocky Mountain Poison and Drug Center received 151 calls for marijuana exposure last year, the first year of retail recreational pot sales. That was up from 88 calls in 2013 and 61 in 2012, the year voters legalized pot. Calls to the Washington Poison Center for marijuana exposures jumped by more than half, from 158 in 2013 to 246 last year.

Travel guide author and marijuana legalization supporter Rick Steves holds a campaign sign in his office in Edmonds, Wash next to a door covered with marijuana leaf-shaped notes from his staff congratulating him on the passage of a referendum legalizing marijuana in the state. In the late-1980s heyday of the "Just Say No" campaign, a man calling himself "Jerry" appeared on a Seattle radio station's midday talk show, using a pseudonym because he was a businessman, afraid of what his customers would think if they heard him criticizing U.S. marijuana laws. A quarter century later, "Jerry" had no problem using his real name - Rick Steves - as one of the main forces behind Washington's successful ballot measure to legalize, regulate and tax marijuana for adults over 21, November 26, 2012. (AP Photo/Elaine Thompson)

Public health experts say they are especially concerned about young children accidentally eating marijuana edibles. Calls involving children nearly doubled in both states: to 48 in Washington involving children 12 or under, and to 45 in Colorado involving children 8 or under.

"There's a bit of a relaxed attitude that this is safe because it's a natural plant, or derived from a natural plant," Dr. Alex Garrard, clinical managing director of the Washington Poison Center. "But this is still a drug. You wouldn't leave Oxycontin lying around on a countertop with kids around, or at least you shouldn't."

Around half of Washington's calls last year involved hospital visits, with most of the patients being evaluated and released from an emergency room, Garrard said. Ten people were admitted to intensive care units - half of them under 20 years old.

Children who wind up going to the hospital for marijuana exposure can find themselves subject to blood tests or spinal taps, Garrard said, because if they seem lethargic and parents don't realize they got into marijuana, doctors might first check for meningitis or other serious conditions.

Dr. Leslie Walker, chief of adolescent medicine at Seattle Children's Hospital, said her facility has had cases where young children needed to be intubated because they were having trouble breathing after consuming marijuana - a terrifically scary experience for parents.

Pot-related calls to Washington's poison center began rising steadily several years ago as medical marijuana dispensaries started proliferating in the state. In 2006, there were just 47 calls. That rose to 150 in 2010 and 162 before actually dropping by a few calls in 2013, a year in which adults could use marijuana but before legal recreational sales had started.

Calls about exposure to marijuana combined with other drugs spiked in Colorado, too. There were 70 such calls last year, up from 39 calls in 2013 and 49 calls in 2012.

Both states saw increases in calls across all age groups. Colorado's biggest increase was among adults over 25 - from 40 in 2013 to 102 calls last year. Washington had a big jump in calls concerning teens, from 40 in 2013 to 61 last year.

Many of the products involved in Washington's exposure cases are found at the state's unregulated medical marijuana dispensaries, but not licensed recreational shops, which are barred from selling marijuana gummy bears or other items that might appeal to children, Garrard said. Medical dispensaries far outnumber legal stores across the state.

Some especially potent marijuana products - such as hash oil - have become more popular in recent years, which could also factor into the increased calls to poison control centers.

The Washington Legislature is working now on proposals for reining in the medical marijuana industry - and limiting what they can sell. Both states have taken steps to try to keep marijuana products away from children, such as requiring child-resistant packaging in licensed stores.

In Denver, authorities charged a couple with child abuse last month, saying their 3-year-old daughter tested positive for marijuana. The couple brought the girl to a hospital after she became sick.

Ben Reagan, a medical marijuana advocate with The Center for Palliative Care in Seattle, said at a recent conference that he had long dealt with parents whose children accidentally got into marijuana. It used to be less likely that they would call an official entity for help, he said.

"Those things have been occurring this whole time," Reagan said. "What you now have is an atmosphere where people are much more comfortable going to the emergency room."

"Before, you'd just look at your buddy and say, `Sorry, dude. You're going to have to deal with it all night,' " he added. "'We're not calling nobody.'"

3

Economics

Sales Begin in US States
December 29, 2013
By Kristen Wyatt

Cheyenne Fox attaches radio frequency tracking tags, required by law, to maturing pot plants inside a grow house, at 3D Cannabis Center, in Denver. Colorado is making final preparations for marijuana sales to begin Jan. 1, a day some are calling "Green Wednesday." 3D Cannabis Center will be open as a recreational retail outlet on New Year's Day, December 31, 2013. (AP Photo/Brennan Linsley)

Colorado and Washington state launched the world's first legal recreational marijuana markets in 2014. Though pot has been sold for three decades at coffee shops in the Netherlands, the two states are the first to regulate and allow a full industry.

Being first to allow growing it, processing it and selling it doesn't come without risks. The states face plenty, from a potential crackdown over a drug that's still illegal under federal law to threats to public health. A look at some of the pitfalls the two states will want to avoid as Big Weed tries to go mainstream:

YOUTH USE:

The U.S. Department of Justice has told the states it won't interfere with state marijuana laws as long as they keep the drug away from those without permission to use it. Top of that list: children. Neither state will allow people under 21 to buy pot.

HEALTH:

Some doctors warn that increased marijuana use will result in more emergency-room visits. There's not enough data to show if that is happening, though some hospitals have reported spikes in child admissions for pot overdoses.

With no Food and Drug Administration oversight, the two states are producing their own product-safety standards to make sure pot is as potent as labeled and doesn't contain harmful molds or other contaminants.

SMUGGLING:

The states have also been told they must keep legal pot out of other states and off federal property.

That's no small task in Western states with huge swaths of federal property, such as parks and ski areas. The states will allow visitors to buy pot, but also warn them about where they can and can't take it.

CRIME:

Legalization opponents say residency requirements won't prevent criminal cartels from setting up straw-man growing operations. The states also have tracking systems to make sure what is grown ends up sold legally. Colorado, however, also allows people to grow pot at home, making it impossible to keep track of where it is coming from and where it's going.

DRIVING:

The states set up marijuana analogies to drunk-driving laws, setting driver blood limits for pot's psychoactive chemical, THC. The laws are new, and it's too soon to say whether legal pot has made highways more dangerous in Colorado and Washington. Both states report seeing more positive driving-high tests, but it's not clear whether that's because of increased driver use or increased testing.

TAXES:

Nobody knows how and at what level to tax marijuana. Too low, and the states won't be able to afford intense regulatory supervision of the industry. Too high, and pot users may stay in the black market.

DEMAND:

Guessing marijuana demand is a tricky proposition. Colorado growers warn that early demand could lead to sky-high prices and shortages, with state production caps still uncertain. In Washington, regulators are taking a new look at supply needs after a recently released study produced a demand estimate that far outstripped earlier guesses.

BANKING:

Marijuana legalization hasn't taken away one black-market aspect for the drug in Colorado and Washington: Cash runs the business. Financial services as simple as checking accounts and credit cards are off-limits because of federal guidance to financial institutions. Colorado officials say they're optimistic the U.S. Treasury Department will loosen those rules next year, but it's unclear what that would look like.

Deb Greene, 65, Cannabis City's first customer, displays her purchase of legal recreational marijuana at the store in Seattle. Greene plans to donate the pot on July 22, 2014, to Museum of History and Industry in Seattle, July 8, 2014. (AP Photo/Elaine Thompson, Pool, File)

Opening Day
January 1, 2014
By Kristen Wyatt

The nation's first recreational pot industry opened in Colorado on Wednesday, January 1, 2014, kicking off a marijuana experiment that will be watched closely around the world. Already, it is attracting people from across the country. Some of the sights in Denver, the Mile High City, on the historic day:

FROM THE JAILHOUSE TO THE POTHOUSE

Less than a year ago, James Aaron Ramsey was serving a brief jail sentence for pot possession. On Wednesday, the 28-year-old musician, having driven from Missouri, was among the first to legally buy weed. He brought a guitar and strummed folk tunes for about 20 people waiting outside one dispensary for sales to begin, as light snow fell at times. "I'm going to frame the receipt when I go home," Ramsey said with a smile. "To remind myself of what might be possible. Legal everywhere."

Others who were waiting in line shared their own pot incarceration stories over coffee and funnel cakes. "They made me go to rehab for marijuana, but I'd get out and see all my underage friends getting drunk all the time," said 24-year-old Brandon Harris, who drove 20 hours from Blanchester, Ohio. "I had to do pee tests, probation visits, the whole thing. Trafficking conviction. Nineteen years old. For a plant, how stupid," he said, shaking his head.

'YOUR GRANDMOTHER'S POT CONNECTION'

Tinted windows on a black limousine idling outside one Denver dispensary showed another side of the newly legal weed market — people eager to try legal marijuana, but not ready to be seen publicly buying it. Addison Morris, owner of Rocky Mountain Mile High Tours, had 10 clients waiting in the limo who paid $295 for four hours of chauffeuring by a "marijuana concierge" who would help them choose strains and edible pot products. "We're your grandmother's pot connection," the 63-year-old said. "We're not the hippie stoners who are going to stand in this cold and party."

Morris said she's booked through the end of February with out-of-state clients. Guests receive samples in designer bags before getting tours. Morris said she's selling discretion. Guests are asked to leave cameras at home. They avoided the crowd at the dispensary, where younger shoppers noshed on funnel cakes and doughnuts from a food truck. Asked if her guests wanted any of the carnival-style treats, Morris recoiled. "Oh God no," she said. "We're going to Whole Foods for breakfast

WILL THERE BE ENOUGH?

Not all marijuana users in Colorado are toasting the dawn of retail sales. Some medical marijuana patients groups say they're worried about supply. That's because the retail inventory for recreational use is coming entirely from the preexisting medical inventory. Many in the industry warned patients to stock up before recreational sales began.

Laura Kriho of the Cannabis Therapy Institute said she worries prices will spike and patients will be left paying more if they're not able to grow their own. "We hope that the focus on recreational doesn't take the focus away from patients who really need this medicine," she said. Their fears weren't misplaced.

Some recreational shops closed early Wednesday because of dwindling supply, and customers grumbled about prices going up. For now, medical patients should have plenty of places to shop. Most of Colorado's 500 or so medical marijuana shops haven't applied to sell recreational pot.

Clerk Havilah Nokes arranges packets of marijuana for sale at Cannabis City on the first day of legal recreational pot sales in Seattle, July 8, 2014. (AP Photo/Elaine Thompson)

AT LEAST THEY OPENED ON TIME

Some Green Wednesday openings were grand, with coffee and live music awaiting early shoppers. Others were more slapdash. As in, not sure until the sun went down New Year's Eve they'd have all their licensing and permitting to open. The Clinic marked the opening of sales by turning on a Bob

Marley CD and hurriedly putting out inventory. Manager Ryan Cook didn't get clearance to open until Tuesday evening. "Never thought we'd be able to get here, but we did it," a bleary-eyed Cook said, hustling around his shop after a long night waiting for new packaging bags that comply with new Colorado regulations.

NOT EVERYONE WAITED

Recreational sales weren't legal until Wednesday, but pot has been legal and free to share in Colorado for more than a year. So marijuana aficionados gathered statewide to mark New Year's Eve with a group toke to count down to when sales begin at 8 a.m. At one party, a 1920s-themed "Prohibition Is Over" gala in Denver, women wore sparkly flapper dresses and men donned suits and suspenders to gather around communal rigs to light up together. A jazz band played, TV monitors showed "The Untouchables" and revelers gathered around a craps table and several card tables. Most of the smoking was outside, but still the air was heavy with marijuana. "This is just pure joy," said David Earley, a 24-year-old marijuana grower form Colorado Springs. "To be able to come out and smoke publicly, it's truly amazing."

THEY BRAVED LONG LINES ...

Two hours. Three hours. Five hours. Marijuana shoppers Wednesday paid a price for shopping on the first day — long waits. Lines snaked down the street outside most pot shops, and the waiting crowds routinely gave a little cheer when shoppers emerged, bags in hand. "How long have we been here?" one marijuana shopper asked his buddies as they emerged from one shop. The sun was setting and the group from Olathe, Kan., hadn't yet checked into their hotel. They'd arrived at the pot shop five hours earlier. The group was smiling, though. "To be able to buy this legally, a much better quality than anything I could get at home, and know it's safe and OK? That's a good thing," said Chris Albrecht, a 25-year-old jazz drummer on his way to a ski vacation in Winter Park.

...AND WORSE WEATHER

Marijuana shoppers were treated to a classic Colorado winter day Wednesday — surprising warmth and sunny skies, interrupted by snow showers and intermittent bursts of frigid wind and rain. Shoppers huddled in gear more frequently seen on ski slopes, then at times peeled off outer layers to T-shirts as they passed the time snacking on hot dogs and sharing stories about marijuana. One of the hungry shoppers was Andre Barr, of Niles, Mich., who picked up a hot dog and shivered during a gusty stretch of his wait. He said the mercurial weather didn't bother him a bit. "This is a huge deal to me,"

Barr said. "At home, I live in fear. Because you will go to jail for the crummiest amount. This feels like liberation."

Freshly packaged cannabis-infused peanut butter cookies are prepared inside Sweet Grass Kitchen, a well-established gourmet marijuana edibles bakery which sells its confections to retail outlets, in Denver, June 19, 2014. (AP Photo/Brennan Linsley, File)

Colorado's Profits: $2 Million
March 10, 2014
By Kristen Wyatt

Colorado made roughly $2 million in marijuana taxes in January, state revenue officials reported Monday, March 10, 2014 in the world's first accounting of the recreational pot business. The tax total reported by the state Department of Revenue indicates $14.02 million worth of recreational pot was sold from 59 businesses. The state collected roughly $2.01 million in taxes.

Colorado legalized pot in 2012, but the commercial sale of marijuana didn't begin until January. Washington state sales begin in coming months. The pot taxes come from 12.9 percent sales taxes and 15 percent excise taxes. Including licensing fees and taxes from Colorado's pre-existing medical marijuana industry, the state collected about $3.5 million from the marijuana industry in January.

That's a relative drop in the bucket for Colorado's roughly $20 billion annual budget, but still a windfall that has numerous interests holding out their hands. By comparison, Colorado made about $2.7 million in liquor excise taxes in January of last year.

Statewide liquor receipts for January 2014 were not yet available Monday. Colorado tax officials say the January marijuana reports were in line with expectations, though they repeatedly said before the figures were reported that they couldn't guess what tax receipts would be. Monday's tax release intensified lobbying over how Colorado should spend its pot money. Budget-writers expect the nascent marijuana industry to be extremely volatile for several years, making lawmakers nervous about where to direct the funds.

Gov. John Hickenlooper already has sent the Legislature a detailed $134 million proposal for spending recreational and medical marijuana money, including new spending on anti-drug messaging to kids and more advertising discouraging driving while high. State police chiefs have asked for more money, too. "The whole world wants to belly up to this trough," said Sen. Pat Steadman, a Denver Democrat who serves on Colorado's budget-writing Joint Budget Committee.

Other countries also are watching Colorado, which has the world's first fully regulated recreational marijuana market. The Netherlands has legal sales of pot but does not allow growing or distribution. Uruguay's marijuana program is still under development. "Colorado's going to help the nation learn what works and what doesn't," said Pat Oglesby, a former congressional tax staffer who now studies marijuana's tax potential at the Chapel Hill, N.C., Center for New Revenue. Colorado has about 160 state-licensed recreational marijuana stores, though local licensing kept some from opening in January.

Only 24 recreational pot shops opened Jan. 1. Oglesby said Colorado's pot sales could grow dramatically in future months as new stores open and marijuana sellers pay more wholesale taxes. Marijuana sellers were allowed a one-time tax-free transfer of medical pot inventory to the recreational market, a caveat that depressed January wholesale tax results. Colorado's pot revenue picture is further complicated by the state's unique budget constraints, known as the Taxpayers' Bill of Rights. The Bill of Rights not only requires voter approval for tax increases, it limits budget-writers when those taxes earn more than the figure posed to voters.

Last year's pot vote guessed that the taxes would produce $70 million a year, and it's unclear what lawmakers can do with tax money that exceeds that figure. Colorado's Joint Budget Committee plans a Wednesday briefing with lawyers to lay out their options for spending pot taxes beyond $70 million. "There probably is a tendency to want to just grab on to this revenue from marijuana and feed my own pet projects, and I don't think it's going to be that simple," said Sen. Kent Lambert, R-Colorado Springs and another committee member. Colorado's 2014-15 budget is under debate now and does not include any anticipated recreational marijuana taxes. Almost the entire haul from recreational pot came from Denver County, where the industry is concentrated. The second- and third-largest counties for medical marijuana, Boulder and El Paso, had no recreational pot shops operating in January.

Boost the Profits
April 24, 2014
By Kristen Wyatt

The federal government has reluctantly agreed to let Colorado be the first state to collect taxes from the legal sale of recreational marijuana, but it also has made clear it doesn't agree with the move and may try to stop it, if isn't tightly controlled.

Instead of keeping a low profile with the money, however, some Colorado lawmakers are trying the bold move of using millions of dollars they've collected so far from pot sales to seek matching funds from the federal government to keep kids off drugs. The plan calls for transferring $3.5 million from the state's marijuana cash fund to its general fund and then sending the same amount to a state department that would apply for a federal match.

Democratic state Sen. Pat Steadman, the measure's sponsor, joked that the bookkeeping move "is what I'm calling money laundering." Supporters say the transfer shouldn't raise any concerns since federal authorities already collect marijuana dollars from the state's medical pot industry and have established guidelines for recreational sales that include keeping the drug away from minors and off federal lands. Moving the money from one fund to another, proponents say, simply acknowledges and avoids potential conflict. Colorado just needs to do "a little two-step" to calm federal nerves, Steadman said, explaining the plan to fellow budget writers.

"We wouldn't want the tainted money to draw a federal match, now, would we?" he added, sarcastically. Skeptics are rolling their eyes. "Colorado is now becoming basically a cartel, a drug cartel," said Sen. Kent Lambert, a Republican on the budget-writing committee, who nonetheless voted in favor. "I don't know what they're trying to do," Lambert said. Maybe "avoid federal scrutiny? I don't think you're going to hide it from the federal government."

The match request would seek funds from the U.S. Centers for Medicare & Medicaid Services "for behavioral health community programs for school-based prevention" of child drug use. Federal Medicaid authorities would have to approve the idea, but it's not immediately clear how the agency would respond.

A CMS spokeswoman declined comment Thursday, April 24, 2014 The idea of sending marijuana revenue to the state's general fund isn't new. Colorado has for years put a 2.9 percent sales tax on medical pot, with the revenue going to the general fund, which routinely sends money along to federal accounts. But the recreational sales industry has created enough cash that lawmakers for the first time will be able to seek a dollar-for-dollar match of pot money with federal money.

Former President Bill Clinton, left, smiles with U.S. Sen. Mark Udall, D-Colo., during a rally at which Clinton urged Coloradans to reelect Udall, as well as Colorado Gov. John Hickenlooper, and other Democratic candidates, in Lakewood, Colo. (AP Photo/Brennan Linsley)

In Washington state, where retail sales haven't yet begun, voters assigned a new dedicated marijuana fund to receive pot taxes and spend the money on health care, drug abuse treatment and education, and marijuana-related research. It's too soon to say whether Washington lawmakers would seek federal matching funds for any of those efforts in the future.

A spokesman for the Colorado department that would seek Medicaid funding insisted that the request to federal authorities will be from general fund dollars. "None of our programs seek funding from marijuana revenues," Marc Williams said in an email.

Williams added that the prevention grants "would likely give preference to those programs operating in school districts or areas where there are a larger number of young, Medicaid-eligible clients." Steadman predicted the federal government would agree to the match. "As long as it is an eligible benefit within the Medicaid program and we're investing state dollars to expand benefits or expand the scope of our program, that's eligible for a federal match," Steadman said this week. "And apparently we should be doing that with general fund dollars, not marijuana tax fund dollars, although in my estimation, all of those dollars are the same shade of green," he said.

The U.S. Department of Justice said in a memo to the states last August that in order to avoid a crackdown on pot laws that flout the federal ban, certain conditions must be met. At the top of the list was keeping marijuana away from minors.

Colorado legalized marijuana for all adults over 21 in 2012, though tax collections didn't start perking up until January, when retail sales began. Projections vary, but legislative budget-writers have projected marijuana taxes and fees will bring Colorado at least $67 million for the fiscal year that begins in July. The budget proposal, which includes a total of $31.4 million in marijuana spending, now faces debate from the full Legislature. Republican Rep. Cheri Gerou predicted a fight. "We're going to be picked apart, once this thing becomes public," she said.

4

Regulations

Changing Pot Laws
June 15, 2015
By Kristen Wyatt

Partygoers dance and smoke pot on the first of two days at the annual 4/20 marijuana festival in Denver, April 19, 2014. (AP Photo/Brennan Linsley, File)

A Colorado man loses custody of his children after getting a medical marijuana card.

The daughter of a Michigan couple growing legal medicinal pot is taken by child-protection authorities after an ex-husband says their plants endangered kids. And police officers in New Jersey visit a home after a 9-year-old mentions his mother's hemp advocacy at school. While the cases were eventually decided in favor of the parents, the incidents underscore a growing dilemma: While a pot plant in the basement may not bring criminal charges in many states, the same plant can become a piece of evidence in child custody or abuse cases.

"The legal standard is always the best interest of the children, and you can imagine how subjective that can get," said Jess Cochrane, who helped found Boston-based Family Law & Cannabis Alliance after finding child-abuse laws have been slow to catch up with pot policy. No data exist to show how often pot use comes up in custody disputes, or how often child-welfare workers intervene in homes where marijuana is used.

But in dozens of interviews with lawyers and officials who work in this area, along with activists who counsel parents on marijuana and child endangerment, the consensus is clear: Pot's growing acceptance is complicating the task of determining when kids are in danger. A failed proposal in the Colorado Legislature this year showed the dilemma. Colorado considers adult marijuana use legal, but pot is still treated like heroin and other Schedule I substances as they are under federal law. As a result, when it comes to defining a drug-endangered child, pot can't legally be in a home where children reside.

Two Democratic lawmakers tried to update the law by saying that marijuana must also be shown to be a harm or risk to children to constitute abuse. But the effort led to angry opposition from both sides — pot-using parents who feared the law could still be used to take their children, and marijuana-legalization opponents who argued that pot remains illegal under federal law and that its very presence in a home threatens kids. After hours of emotional testimony, lawmakers abandoned the effort as too complicated. Among the teary-eyed moms at the hearing was Moriah Barnhart, who moved to the Denver area from Tampa, Florida, in search of a cannabis-based treatment for a daughter with brain cancer. "We moved here across the country so we wouldn't be criminals. But all it takes is one neighbor not approving of what we're doing, one police officer who doesn't understand, and the law says I'm a child abuser," Barnhart said. Supporters vow to try again to give law enforcement some definitions about when the presence of drugs could harm children, even if the kids don't use it.

"There are people who are very reckless with what they're doing, leaving marijuana brownies on the coffee table or doing hash oil extraction that might blow the place up. Too often with law enforcement, they're just looking at the legality of the behavior and not how it is affecting the children," said Jim Gerhardt of the Colorado Drug Investigators Association, which supported the bill. Colorado courts are wading into the question of when adult pot use endangers kids. The state Court of Appeals in 2010 sided with a marijuana-using dad who lost visitation rights though he never used the drug around his daughter. The court reversed a county court's decision that the father couldn't have unsupervised visitation until passing a drug test, saying that a parent's marijuana use when away from his or her children doesn't suggest any risk of child harm.

But child-endangerment standards remain murky in Colorado, with wide disparities in how local child-protection officers and law enforcement approach pot, said Rob Corry, a Denver lawyer who successfully argued the father's custody appeal. Corry, who helped Colorado's 2012 campaign to legalize recreational marijuana, said the main thrust of the effort was to treat pot like alcohol. "Think of brewing beer. You've got a constitutional right to do it.

There's nothing wrong with it. Marijuana should be just as simple — you just keep it on a high shelf, right next to your vodka. But in practice, this is not how law enforcement treats marijuana," he said. In the absence of legal guidelines, a growing network of blogs counsel parents in how to deal with police or child-protection agencies concerned about parental marijuana use, including one, Ladybud, run by legal-pot activist Diane Fornbacher. She said she moved to Colorado this year after child-protection workers visited her family in New Jersey after a teacher alerted officials when her son mentioned hemp — pot's non-hallucinogenic cousin — at school. "They said, 'We're just here to help.' Emotionally, my brain was like, 'My kids! My kids!' My mama bear instinct kicked in," she said.

Smaller-dose pot-infused brownies are divided and packaged at The Growing Kitchen, in Boulder, Colo. Colorado health officials want to ban many edible forms of marijuana, including brownies, cookies and most candies, limiting sales of pot-infused food to lozenges and some liquids, September 26, 2014. (AP Photo/Brennan Linsley, File)

The need for better standards about when marijuana endangers kids is growing by the day, said Maria Green, a Lansing, Michigan, mother who lost custody of her infant daughter for three months last year.

Green grows pot to treat her husband's epilepsy, and though Michigan's medical marijuana law states parents shall not be denied custody or visitation with a child for following the statute, a legal dispute with her ex-husband led to her daughter being placed with a grandparent until it was resolved.

The ex-husband who brought the complaint declined an interview until talking with his lawyer. "I never in a million years thought that they were going to take my daughter," Green said. "I know that there's a place for child protection, but I would love to see it used to protect kids from being actually hurt."

Edible Pot Ban
October 20, 2014
By Kristen Wyatt

Colorado health authorities suggested banning many forms of edible marijuana, including brownies and cookies, then whipsawed away from the suggestion Monday, October 20, 2014, after it went public. The Colorado Department of Public Health and Environment told state pot regulators they should limit edible pot on shelves to hard lozenges and tinctures, which are a form of liquid pot that can be added to foods and drinks.

The suggestion sparked marijuana industry outrage and legal concerns from a regulatory workgroup that met Monday to review the agency's suggestion. Colorado's 2012 marijuana-legalization measure says retail pot is legal in all forms. "If the horse wasn't already out of the barn, I think that would be a nice proposal for us to put on the table," said Karin McGowan, the department's deputy executive director.

Talking to reporters after the workgroup reviewed the department's proposal, McGowan insisted the edibles ban was just one of several proposals under review by pot regulators.

Lawmakers have ordered state pot regulators to require pot-infused food and drink to have a distinct look when they are out of the packaging. The order came after concerns about the proliferation of pot-infused treats that many worry could be accidentally eaten by children.

Statewide numbers are not available, but one hospital in the Denver area has reported nine cases of children being admitted after accidentally eating pot. It is not clear whether those kids ate commercially packaged pot products or homemade items such as marijuana brownies.

The Health Department's recommendation was one of several made to marijuana regulators. "We need to know what is in our food," said Gina Carbone of the advocacy group Smart Colorado, which says edible pot shouldn't be allowed if it can't be identified out of its packaging.

Marijuana industry representatives insisted that marking pot won't prevent accidental ingestions. "There is only so much we can do as manufacturers to prevent a child from putting a product in their mouth," said Bob Eschino of Incredibles, which makes marijuana-infused chocolates. Even health officials worried that an edibles ban would not stop people from making homemade pot treats, with possibly more dangerous results. "Edibles are very, very popular.

And I do worry that people are going to make their own. They're not going to know what they're doing," said Dr. Lalit Bajaj of Children's Hospital Colorado.

The meeting came a few days after Denver police released a video about the danger of possible Halloween candy mix-ups. "Some marijuana edibles can be literally identical to their name-brand counterparts," the department warned in a statement, urging parents to toss candies they don't recognize.

The edible pot workgroup meets again in November before sending a recommendation to Colorado lawmakers next year. The revised edible rule is to be in place by 2016.

Driving While Stoned
September 1, 2014
By Joan Lowy

As states liberalize their marijuana laws, public officials and safety advocates worry that more drivers high on pot will lead to a big increase in traffic deaths. Researchers, though, are divided on the question.

Studies of marijuana's effects show that the drug can slow decision-making, decrease peripheral vision and impede multitasking, all of which are critical driving skills. But unlike with alcohol, drivers high on pot tend to be aware that they are impaired and try to compensate by driving slowly, avoiding risky actions such as passing other cars, and allowing extra room between vehicles. On the other hand, combining marijuana with alcohol appears to eliminate the pot smoker's exaggerated caution and seems to increase driving impairment beyond the effects of either substance alone. "We see the legalization of marijuana in Colorado and Washington as a wake-up call for all of us in highway safety," said Jonathan Adkins, executive director of Governors Highway Safety Association, which represents state highway safety offices. "We don't know enough about the scope of marijuana-impaired driving to call it a big or small problem. But anytime a driver has their ability impaired, it is a problem." Colorado and Washington are the only states that allow retail sales of marijuana for recreational use.

Amy Ford, Director of Communications for the Colorado Dept. of Transportation, speaks during a news conference at which she announced the launch of a new "Drive High, Get A DUI" campaign, a TV-and-radio attempt to remind drivers that newly legal weed should be treated like alcohol and not consumed before driving, at the Colorado State Patrol Training Academy, in Golden, Colo., March 6, 2014. (AP Photo/Brennan Linsley)

Efforts to legalize recreational marijuana are underway in Alaska, Massachusetts, New York, Oregon and the District of Columbia. Twenty-three states and the nation's capital permit marijuana use for medical purposes. It is illegal in all states to drive while impaired by marijuana. Colorado, Washington and Montana have set an intoxication threshold of 5 parts per billion of THC, the psychoactive ingredient in pot, in the blood. A few other states have set intoxication thresholds, but most have not set a specific level. In Washington, there was a jump of nearly 25 percent in drivers testing positive for marijuana in 2013 — the first full year after legalization — but no corresponding increase in car accidents or fatalities. What worries highway safety experts are cases like that of New York teenager Joseph Beer, who in October 2012 smoked marijuana, climbed into a Subaru Impreza with four friends and drove more than 100 mph before losing control.

The car crashed into trees with such force that the vehicle split in half, killing his friends. Beer pleaded guilty to aggravated vehicular homicide and was sentenced last week to 5 years to 15 years in prison. A prosecutor blamed the crash on "speed and weed," but a Yale University Medical School expert on drug abuse who testified at the trial said studies of marijuana and crash risk are "highly inconclusive." Some studies show a two- or three-fold increase, while others show none, said Dr. Mehmet Sofuoglu.

State trooper Carrie Jackson completes a roadside Drug Influence Evaluation sheet on a clipboard, during a several week long Drug Recognition Expert class at the Colorado State Patrol Training Academy, in Golden, Colo., March 6, 2014. (AP Photo/Brennan Linsley)

Some studies even showed less risk if someone was marijuana positive, he testified. Teenage boys and young men are the most likely drivers to smoke pot and the most likely drivers to have an accident regardless of whether they're high, he said. "Being a teenager, a male teenager, and being involved in reckless behavior could explain both at the same time — not necessarily marijuana causing getting into accidents, but a general reckless behavior leading to both conditions at the same time," he told jurors. In 2012, just over 10 percent of high school seniors said they had smoked pot before driving at least once in the prior two weeks, according to Monitoring the Future, an annual University of Michigan survey of 50,000 middle and high school students. Nearly twice as many male students as female students said they had smoked marijuana before driving.

A roadside survey by the National Highway Traffic Safety Administration in 2007 found 8.6 percent of drivers tested positive for THC, but it's not possible to say how many were high at the time because drivers were tested only for the presence of drugs, not the amount. A marijuana high generally peaks within a half hour and dissipates within three hours, but THC can linger for days in the bodies of habitual smokers. Inexperienced pot smokers are likely to be more impaired than habitual smokers, who develop a tolerance. Some studies show virtually no driving impairment in habitual smokers.

Two recent studies that used similar data to assess crash risk came to opposite conclusions. Columbia University researchers compared drivers who tested positive for marijuana in the roadside survey with state drug and alcohol tests of drivers killed in crashes. They found that marijuana alone increased the likelihood of being involved in a fatal crash by 80 percent. But because the study included states where not all drivers are tested for alcohol and drugs, a majority of drivers in fatal crashes were excluded, possibly skewing the results.

Co-Founder Kevin Sabet speaks during the closing ceremony of the National Association of Drug Court Professionals' 20th Annual Training Conference, at the Anaheim Convention Center in Anaheim, CA., May 31, 2014. (Eric Reed/AP Images for The National Association of Drug Court Professionals)

Also, the use of urine tests rather than blood tests in some cases may overestimate marijuana use and impairment. A Pacific Institute for Research and Evaluation study used the roadside survey and data from nine states that test more than 80 percent of drivers killed in crashes.

When adjusted for alcohol and driver demographics, the study found that otherwise sober drivers who tested positive for marijuana were slightly less likely to have been involved in a crash than drivers who tested negative for all drugs. "We were expecting a huge impact," said Eduardo Romano, lead author of the study, "and when we looked at the data from crashes we're not seeing that much."

But Romano said his study may slightly underestimate the risk and that marijuana may lead to accidents caused by distraction.

Many states do not test drivers involved in a fatal crash for drugs unless there is reason to suspect impairment. Even if impairment is suspected, if the driver tests positive for alcohol, there may be no further testing because alcohol alone may be enough to bring criminal charges.

Testing procedures also vary from state to state. "If states legalize marijuana, they must set clear limits for impairment behind the wheel and require mandatory drug testing following a crash," said Deborah Hersman, former chairman of the National Transportation Safety Board.

"Right now we have a patchwork system across the nation regarding mandatory drug testing following highway crashes."

The legalization of recreational marijuana in two states — Colorado and Washington — and medical marijuana in more than 20 others has raised concern that there will be more drivers stoned behind the wheel. What's not clear is whether that will translate into an increase in fatal crashes. Five things to know about marijuana and driving:

WHAT WE KNOW

While marijuana users can perform simple tasks well while they are high, brain imaging has shown they have to use more of their brain to do so. Their reaction times are slower, peripheral vision is decreased and multitasking impeded. As a result, when sudden or surprising things occur to complicate those tasks — such as when a pedestrian steps in front of a car — they cannot respond as well. On the other hand, marijuana users tend to be aware they are impaired and try to compensate for it.

WHAT WE DON'T KNOW

It's not clear how much marijuana use contributes to crash risk. Some studies have found that marijuana can double crash risk, but others have found virtually no increase.

HOW HIGH IS TOO HIGH?

Traces of THC, the psychoactive ingredient in marijuana, can be detected in the blood of some habitual marijuana users days or weeks after they last used the drug, making it hard to use blood tests to discern a current level of impairment.

Most states haven't set a THC threshold for impairment, but Colorado and Washington have settled on an intoxication blood level of 5 parts per billion. There's no roadside test for THC like those for alcohol, but some states are experimenting with a saliva test.

REAL-WORLD EXPERIENCE

In 2013, the first full year after Washington state legalized pot, nearly 25 percent more drivers tested positive for marijuana than before legalization.

But there has been no corresponding jump in accidents or arrests for intoxicated driving. A University of Colorado Medical School study found that the share of drivers involved in fatal motor vehicle crashes in Colorado who tested positive for marijuana more than doubled between 1994 and 2011. A National Safety Council study looked at the prevalence of drivers involved in fatal crashes who tested positive for marijuana in 12 states from 1992 to 2009, before and after implementing medical marijuana laws. Only three states showed an increase — California, Hawaii and Washington — and those appeared to be a one-time increase possibly associated with differences in testing.

WHAT NEXT?

The National Highway Traffic Safety Administration is conducting research to get a better idea of how pot affects driving. NHTSA and Washington state officials have also teamed up to assess change in marijuana use by drivers before and after the state allowed retail sale of the drug, with results due next year.

Doing Business
February 14, 2014
By Pete Yost

Others have a keen interest, too, in a regulated financial pipeline for an industry that is just emerging from the underground. Marijuana businesses that can't use banks may have too much cash they can't safely put away, leaving them vulnerable to criminals. And governments that allow marijuana sales want a channel to receive taxes.

The Obama administration gave banks a road map for conducting transactions with legal marijuana sellers so these new businesses can stash away savings, make payroll and pay taxes like any other enterprise. It's not clear banks will get on board. Guidance issued by the Justice and Treasury departments is the latest step by the federal government toward enabling a legalized marijuana industry to operate in states that approve it. The intent is to make banks feel more comfortable working with marijuana businesses that are licensed and regulated, February 14, 2014. (AP Photo)

But a leading financial services trade group immediately expressed misgivings and others, too, said the guidelines don't go far enough in protecting banks. "After a series of red lights, we expected this guidance to be a yellow one," said Don Childears, president and CEO of the Colorado Bankers Asociation. "This isn't close to that. At best, this amounts to 'serve these customers at your own risk' and it emphasizes all of the risks. This light is red." Washington and Colorado in 2012 became the first states to approve recreational use of marijuana.

A group is hoping to make Alaska the third state in the nation to do so. Currently, processing money from marijuana sales puts federally insured banks at risk of drug racketeering charges, so they've refused to open accounts for marijuana-related businesses. Friday's move was designed to let financial institutions serve such businesses while ensuring that they know their customers' legitimacy and remain obligated to report possible criminal activity, said the Treasury Department's Financial Crimes Enforcement Network, or FinCEN.

But in response, the American Bankers Association said "guidance or regulation doesn't alter the underlying challenge for banks. As it stands, possession or distribution of marijuana violates federal law, and banks that provide support for those activities face the risk of prosecution and assorted sanctions."

The group says banks will only be comfortable serving marijuana businesses if federal prohibitions on the drug are changed in law. Denny Eliason, a lobbyist for the Washington Bankers Association, said it will take some time before banks decide whether to take advantage of the guidance. He called it a good first step, but said it sets forth a complicated process for the banks to follow — for example, by filing suspicious activity reports designated "marijuana limited" in the case of business that seem to be complying with the rules, and "marijuana priority" for those acting questionably. "They'll have to have a real awareness of the activities of their customers," he said.

State banking regulators in Colorado and Washington appear to believe that mainly small and medium-sized banks will be interested in handling financial transactions with legal marijuana stores, not the big ones, a FinCEN official said, speaking only on condition of anonymity to talk about internal deliberations. "This is a decision that each financial institution needs to make on its own," the official said. "We feel quite comfortable that we have acted within the scope of our authority" and therefore don't expect legal challenges to the new procedures. FinCEN writes the rules that U.S. financial institutions must follow to help protect the system from money laundering and the financing of terrorism.

The office said it expects financial institutions to perform thorough customer due diligence on marijuana businesses and file reports that will be valuable to law enforcement. Under the guidance, banks must review state license applications for marijuana customers, request information about the business, develop an understanding of the types of products to be sold and monitor publicly available sources for any negative information about the business.

Asked about the conflict in federal and state laws on marijuana use, the official said the agency sought to balance competing interests. One of them is the concern about having so much cash on the street without an ability to get those funds into the safety of a bank. The guidance provided the banks with more than 20 "red flags" that may indicate a violation of federal law. Among them: if a business receives substantially more revenue than its local competitors, deposits more cash than is in line with the amount of marijuana-related revenue it is reporting for federal and state tax purposes, or experiences a surge in activity by third parties offering goods or services such as equipment suppliers or shipping services.

If a marijuana-related business is seen engaging in international or interstate activity, such as the receipt of cash deposits from locations outside the state, that's a red flag, too. It has been difficult for legal marijuana sellers to operate without banks in the mix.

"It's not just banks that are wary about handling our money, it's everybody — security businesses, lawyers, you name it, no one wants to take the risk of taking our money," said Caitlin McGuire, owner of Breckenridge Cannabis Club in Breckenridge, Colo. McGuire's shop had an account with a local credit union for years, but the credit union cut them off last year. "They basically told us they wanted to keep our accounts, but it was too big of a risk. They were questioned by their auditors, 'Why do you have this marijuana account?' It just ended up being too much for them." The pot shop now pays its bills with money orders and cash. It's not easy, McGuire said. "It's made it very difficult to pay our bills, to pay our employees, to pay our taxes, to do anything."

5

The Stoner Stereotype

The Marijuana Industry
September 17, 2014
Kristen Wyatt

Seth Clanton waits in line outside of Cannabis City Tuesday in Seattle, on the first day that sales of recreational pot became legal in the state, July 8, 2014. (AP Photo/Elaine Thompson)

Tired of Cheech & Chong pot jokes and ominous anti-drug campaigns, the marijuana industry and activists are starting an ad blitz in Colorado aimed at promoting moderation and the safe consumption of pot.

To get their message across, they are skewering some of the old Drug War-era ads that focused on the fears of marijuana, including the famous "This is your brain on drugs" fried-egg ad from the 1980s. They are planning posters, brochures, billboards and magazine ads to caution consumers to use the drug responsibly and warn tourists and first-timers about the potential to get sick from accidentally eating too much medical-grade pot. "So far, every campaign designed to educate the public about marijuana has relied on fear-mongering and insulting marijuana users," said Mason Tvert, spokesman for the Marijuana Policy Project, the nation's biggest pot-policy advocacy group. The MPP plans to unveil a billboard on Wednesday on a west Denver street where many pot shops are located that shows a woman slumped in a hotel room with the tagline: "Don't let a candy bar ruin your vacation."

It's an allusion to Maureen Dowd, a New York Times columnist who got sick from eating part of a pot-infused candy bar on a visit to write about pot. The campaign is a direct response to the state's post-legalization marijuana-education efforts. One of them is intended to prevent stoned driving and shows men zoning out while trying to play basketball, light a grill or hang a television.

Many in the industry said the ads showed stereotypical stoners instead of average adults. Even more concerning to activists is a youth-education campaign that relies on a human-sized cage and the message, "Don't Be a Lab Rat," along with warnings about pot and developing brains.

The cage in Denver has been repeatedly vandalized. At least one school district rejected the traveling exhibit, saying it was well-intentioned but inappropriate. "To me, that's not really any different than Nancy Reagan saying 'Just Say No,'" said Tim Cullen, co-owner of four marijuana dispensaries and a critic of the "lab rat" campaign, referring to the former first lady's effort to combat drug use. A spokesman for the state Health Department welcomed the industry's ads, and defended the "lab rat" campaign. "It's been effective in starting a conversation about potential risks to youth from marijuana," Mark Salley said. The dueling campaigns come at a time when the industry is concerned about inexperienced consumers using edible pot.

The popularity of edibles surprised some in the industry when legal-marijuana retail sales began in January. Edible pot products have been blamed for at least one death, of a college student who jumped to his death in Denver in March after consuming six times the recommended dose of edible marijuana. The headlines, including Dowd's experience, have been enough for the industry to promote moderation with edible pot. "I think the word has gotten out that you need to be careful with edibles," said Steve Fox, head of the Denver-based Council for Responsible Cannabis Regulation. The group organized the "First Time 5" campaign, which cautions that new users shouldn't eat more than 5 milligrams of marijuana's psychoactive ingredient, or half a suggested serving.

The campaign warns users that edible pot can be much more potent than the marijuana they're smoking — and that the pot-infused treats on store shelves are much stronger than homemade brownies they may recall eating. The advocacy ads tackle anti-drug messaging from year past. Inside pictures of old TV sets are images from historic ads.

Along with the fried-egg one is an image from one ad of a father finding his son's drug stash and demanding to know who taught him to use it. The kid answers: "You, all right! I learned it by watching you!" The print ad concludes, "Decades of fear-mongering and condescending anti-marijuana ads have not taught us anything about the substance or made anyone safer." It then directs viewers to consumeresposibly.org, which is patterned after the alcohol industry's "Drink Responsibly" campaign. Marijuana activists plan to spend $75,000 by year's end and eventually expand it to Washington state, where pot is also legal.

The New Edible Pot
August 1, 2014
By Colin Jeffery

Kevin Nelson, of Bellingham, Wash., holds a sign that reads "Drug War Ends Here," outside Top Shelf Cannabis in Bellingham, Wash. on the first day of legal pot sales in the state, July 8, 2014. (AP Photo/Ted S. Warren)

Marijuana can go in more than brownies and cookies. And the dizzying variety of foods that can be infused with the drug is complicating matters for Colorado regulators who want to make sure pot-infused edibles and drinks won't be confused with regular foods.

A first meeting Friday August 1, 2014, of edible marijuana makers, state regulators and pot critics ran into controversy early. Many seem to agree that pot cookies and candies should come with identifiable markers or colors. But what about marijuana-infused honey? Or pasta sauce? Colorado opened recreational marijuana to adults over 21 in January. Since then, sales have boomed for edible pot, considered a tastier or healthier alternative to smoking weed. Now regulators are looking for ways to make sure no one accidentally eats or drinks the drug.

"I want to know what's a Duncan Hines brownie and what's a marijuana brownie, just by looking at it. Whether you're 5 or 50, people need to know what that is," said Rep. Jonathan Singer, D-Longmont, who sponsored the new law requiring edible marijuana to be "clearly identifiable."

Marijuana food and drink makers helping write those regulations didn't seem to oppose stamps or marks on easily-marked products like hard candies or chocolate bars. But the workgroup tripped up when contemplating all the varieties of foods that can be infused with marijuana's psychoactive ingredient, THC. Liquids, powdered drink mixes, even meats and cereals can be infused with THC.

"How are we going to be able to make these edibles identifiable to the public, so that they know this is marijuana? This is a very, very heavy lift," said Gina Carbone, a volunteer for SMART Colorado, a group critical of the marijuana industry. Carbone suggested that some edible marijuana products — such as lollipops or gummy bears — shouldn't be allowed for commercial sale because they are likely to appeal to kids. "We're going to allow every edible imaginable, versus another approach where edibles are regulated," Carbone said after suggesting some products should be taken off store shelves. But the suggestion got a sour reaction from industry operators and Singer, all of whom argued that the black market already produces unregulated edibles, and that banning food people want to eat is a bad idea.

"We're here to identify products, not to limit items on the market," said Jaime Lewis of Mountain Medicine, which makes pot-infused sweets such as pie bars and chocolate-covered pretzels. The panel made no decisions Friday and plans to meet twice more before making a recommendation to the Colorado Legislature in February.

The meeting came a day after Colorado adopted emergency edible-pot rules aimed at making it easier for consumers to tell how much pot they're eating. The new rules require edible products to be easily divisible into "servings" of 10 mg of THC, about the amount in a medium-sized joint. Colorado's rules already require edible pot to be sold in "servings" of 10 milligrams of THC. But many consumers have complained they can't tell what a serving is and eat too much of a heavily dosed product. Those stronger-dosed edibles are holdovers from the medical pot marketplace, where sellers say consumers who have built up strong tolerances won't buy anything that has a dosage less than 100 milligrams of THC.

Novices to Marijuana
October 9, 2014
By Kristen Wyatt

Recreational marijuana sellers are reaching out to novice cannabis users with a raft of edible products that impart a milder buzz and make it easy for inexperienced customers to find a dose they won't regret taking. In many ways, the marketing shift is the pot-industry equivalent of selling beer and wine alongside higher-alcohol options such as whiskey and vodka. "No one buys a handle of Jim Beam and thinks they should drink all of that in one sitting," said Tim Cullen, owner of two Denver-area marijuana dispensaries.

A caregiver picks out a marijuana bud for a patient at a marijuana dispensary in Denver, September 18, 2012. (AP Photo/Ed Andrieski)

"But people do want to eat an entire cookie, an entire piece of chocolate. So these products allow you to do that and not have a miserable experience." Nine months into Colorado's recreational pot experiment, retailers have good reason to court new users. A market study released in July suggested 40 percent of customers in Denver-area recreational marijuana shops are tourists. That figure spikes to 90 percent in ski towns such as Aspen or Breckenridge.

Tourists cannot shop in medical-marijuana dispensaries, so many of those customers may be buying legal weed for the first time. New on the shelves in Colorado's recreational pot shops is the "Rookie Cookie," a marijuana-infused confection that contains 10 milligrams of marijuana's psychoactive ingredient, THC.

Tripp Keber, head of Denver-based Dixie Elixirs & Edibles, which makes pot-infused drinks, foods and other items, stands inside one of his edibles production kitchens at his manufacturing facility in Denver, September 25, 2014. (AP Photo/Brennan Linsley)

That's a low enough dose that most adults wouldn't be too impaired to drive a car, defined in Colorado as a blood level of five parts per billion of THC. Then there's a new marijuana-infused soda that's 15 times weaker than the company's best-known soda. The Dixie One watermelon cream soda contains 5 milligrams of THC — half of what the state considers a serving size — and is billed as "great for those who are new to THC or don't like to share." The wave of lighter choices comes as the new industry tries to pivot away from products aimed at frequent, heavy pot users to newer customers who weren't interested in the drug when it was illegal.

"For a long time, the medical market was a race to the strongest edibles. Now it's a new market, and people want something that won't get them so inebriated they're not functional," said Holden Sproul of the Growing Kitchen, which makes the "Rookie Cookie" and is phasing out some of its stronger offerings. There's no publicly available data on which products are selling.

But interviews with dispensary owners and marijuana producers suggest the lighter products are booming. "We still get people walking in here saying,

'What's the strongest thing?' But more and more they're asking about flavor, the experience, the whole nine yards," Cullen said.

In Washington state, where sales of edibles are just beginning in recreational pot shops, some of the first licensed edible-makers are taking a similar approach.

The entire product line at Db3 Inc. in Seattle is based around the idea that consumers can control the effect they want — an idea based in part on market research that suggested people often had bad experiences because they over-consumed marijuana edibles.

Among the products Db3 hopes to get on retail shelves in the coming weeks are liquid drops that can be added to beverages in precise amounts. "We recognize there are going to be a lot of nontraditional users coming into the market, or people who have used in the past a long time ago and who are just getting back into it," said Patrick Devlin, one of the company's founders.

There's more than market share at stake. Marijuana-legalization activists want to tamp down stories about pot users who got sick after eating potent medical-grade cannabis, an experience so common it seems everyone in Denver knows someone who endured it. Most serious was the March death of a college student who had never tried pot before visiting Denver for spring break.

The man ate a single cookie that contained 65 milligrams of THC then jumped to his death from a hotel balcony after his friends said he started acting erratically. And New York Times columnist Maureen Dowd famously wrote in June of trying a marijuana-infused candy bar, after which she "lay curled up in a hallucinatory state for the next eight hours." Colorado dispensaries have launched a "First Time 5" campaign of posters to encourage new users to take a 5 milligram half-dose of marijuana to make sure they don't overdo it.

A marijuana advocacy group has taken out billboards and magazine ads with the tagline "Start Low, Go Slow."

At least one marketing expert warned that pot producers need to be careful not to claim their products won't cause intoxication. "Is it too early in the industry to go claiming what's a low dose and what's a medium dose?" asked Claire Kaufmann of Portland, Oregon, who consults for manufacturers and runs a "Rebranding Cannabis" blog. "We want to create a place for new consumers in our industry. We just need to be aware that we don't get ahead of the science."

Celebrating Marijuana
August 1, 2014
By Kristen Wyatt

Marijuana joined roses and dahlias Friday August 1, 2014 in blue ribbon events at the nation's first county fair to allow pot competitions.

The first weekend of August's Denver County Fair includes a 21-and-over "Pot Pavilion" where winning entries for plants, bongs, edible treats and clothes made from hemp are on display. There is no actual weed at the fairgrounds. Instead, fairgoers will see photos of the competing pot plants and marijuana-infused foods. A sign near the entry warns patrons not to consume pot at the fair.

David Ittel poses outside his Brew & Grow shop in Chicago store where he has sold indoor gardening supplies for three decades in Illinois and Wisconsin. As Illinois and other states legalize medical marijuana, there's one stage in the process that nobody wants to talk about, October 6, 2014. (AP Photo/M. Spencer Green)

A speed joint-rolling contest uses oregano, not pot. The only real stuff allowed at the event? Doritos, to be used in the munchie eating contest. Organizers say the marijuana categories this year — which come with the debut of legal recreational marijuana in Colorado — add a fun twist on Denver's already-quirky county fair, which includes a drag queen pageant and a contest for dioramas made with Peeps candies. "We've been selling tickets to people from all over the world, and we keep hearing they want to come see the pot," said Dana Cain, who helped organize Denver County's first fair three years ago.

This year's event is expected to draw 20,000 people. Judges considered only the quality of individual marijuana plants, not potency or the merits of drugs produced by the plants. "It's more like a rose competition than anything," said Russel Wise, a pot grower who entered three plants and a marijuana-infused baklava treat. Other Colorado contests — patterned after Amsterdam's famed Cannabis Cup — gauge drug quality and flavor. Edible products did require tasting.

A secret panel of judges sampled brownies and other treats earlier this month at an undisclosed location. "At first the judges were eating them all, but by the end they were really feeling it, so they just tasted them and spit them out," Cain said with a laugh. "We offered them cabs home." The winning brownie was made with walnuts and dark chocolate. Top prize was $20 and a blue ribbon. The fair already has a green ribbon — awarded for using environmentally conscious methods.

For the handmade bong contest, three industry insiders judged 17 entries for craftsmanship, creativity — and functionality. "It has to be something special, something you'd want to use," said judge Robert Folse, who works at a pot dispensary as a "budtender," sort of a sommelier for marijuana. It's too soon to say whether marijuana contests will spread to other state fairs. Officials in Routt County, in western Colorado, voted last year to ban marijuana from the county fair.

Colorado State Fair organizers have expressed no interest in marijuana competition. California holds an Emerald Cup at the fairgrounds in Sonoma County, where guests with medical clearance are able to sample the drug. That contest is held at the fairgrounds but isn't a part of the county fair.

Marijuana Dining
December 2, 2014
By Kristen Wyatt

Acclaimed chef Chris Lanter is talking to a crowd of eager foodies through a demo on cooking with marijuana. As he prepares steak au poivre, he describes how to deglaze the pan with pot-infused brandy. How to pair marijuana with fine foods. How to make marijuana's skunky tang work for a dish, not ruin it.

One catch - there's no actual weed at his demonstration. Marijuana aficionados paid $250 for a weekend-long celebration of marijuana and food, yet state and city regulations prohibit any "open and public" use of the drug, even at licensed businesses holding private events. It's a strange dichotomy.

Marijuana smokers enter the Cannabis Culture Headquarters in Vancouver, British Columbia. Vancouver is in the marijuana-friendly corner of Canada, and it's hard to miss, February 23, 2010. (AP Photo/Jae C. Hong)

The nascent marijuana industry in Colorado is moving well beyond just pot brownies. Dispensaries are doing a booming trade in cookbooks, savory pot foods and frozen takeout dishes that incorporate the drug. But for now, halting attempts at creating a marijuana dining scene have had mixed results. Colorado may have legalized marijuana, but it still prohibits "on-site consumption," a caveat aimed at preventing Amsterdam-style coffee shops where pot can be purchased and consumed in the same place. Recreational or medical marijuana is now legal in 23 states and Washington, DC. - though each state prohibits on-site consumption and pot sales in bars or restaurants.

As Colorado's recreational industry nears its first anniversary, authorities increasingly are cracking down on attempts to push the pot-dining envelope. The city of Denver, where the marijuana industry is concentrated, wrote 668 tickets for "open and public consumption" through September, up from 117 the year before, when marijuana was legal, but sales were not. And the county that includes Colorado Springs is trying to crack down on so-called "smoke-easys," or private clubs that allow marijuana use, sometimes paired with refreshments. Even private events at restaurants aren't safe. Denver authorities are using permit codes and alcohol laws to fine and even press charges against people trying to throw private events at which pot foods are served.

The result has been that chefs interested in infusing foods with pot, or pairing regular dishes with certain strains thought to accent a particular flavor, are unable to try it outside catered events at private homes. Even chefs who will talk publicly about doing "medicated" catered house parties, like Lanter, are skittish about sharing details. "There's so much potential here, and the interest is unbelievable.

But right now, everybody's kind of scared to be doing it," says Lanter, owner and executive chef at Aspen's tony Cache Cache restaurant. Which isn't to say folks aren't experimenting with the limits of the law. A bed-and-breakfast in Denver offers guests samples of cannabis strains alongside regular breakfast dishes. Guests at The Adagio get marijuana samples at daily happy hours, too, where strains of pot are paired with crudites and bacon-wrapped chicken bites, complete with tasting note presentations from growers. "It's a way to bring our guests together and move away from campy, stereotypical pot foods," says Joel Schneider, CEO of the MaryJane Group, which operates two marijuana-friendly hotels. But Schneider has to be careful.

The pot he hands out goes only to paying hotel guests over 21, allowing him to argue the tastings aren't public. His attempts to do more public events have been shut down by police. He also avoids serving any foods that contain marijuana, something that could land him a criminal citation. Chefs worried about criminal charges point to Amy Dannemiller, owner of Denver-based Edible Events, which helped organized last summer's cannabis-friendly concerts with the Colorado Symphony Orchestra. Dannemiller, known professionally as Jane West, recently pleaded guilty to an alcohol charge related to her upscale bring-your-own marijuana parties.

The events were held at tony bars and art galleries, where guests paid $95 or more for an open bar and a place to use marijuana. Dannemiller received a deferred six-month sentence. Now she is pushing for a new law to clarify how marijuana can be consumed at adults-only events. Foodies interested in marijuana dining insist the law eventually will change to permit cannabis dining.

They say the drug pairs well with food and that public acceptance will grow once people stop associating cannabis dining with brownies and junk-food munchies. Back at Lanter's event in Aspen, one attendee had good reason for optimism about fine dining with cannabis. Marcy DiSalvo attended the first iteration of Aspen's noted Food & Wine Classic, held in 1983, and found similarities with this year's cannabis cooking celebration, called the Cannabis Grand Cru. "You know, it was a lot like this - just a couple hundred people getting together to talk about their love of food. And wine. Or in this case, marijuana," DiSalvo said. "This is classy. It's done right. It's not a bunch of stoners; it's people with a gourmet approach."

6

The Perception of Marijuana Across the Country

A Shift in Public Opinion
April 3, 2014
By Kristen Wyatt

Minnesota Gov. Mark Dayton delivers his State of the State address before a joint session of the Legislature in St. Paul, Minn. Democrats who control the Minnesota Legislature can brag about key accomplishments in the just-completed session, including a big boost in the minimum wage and a tougher statewide anti-bullying law. But they needed and got help from Republicans to push through $1.1 billion in spending on construction projects, major tax relief and legalized medical marijuana, April 30, 2014. (AP Photo/Tom Olmscheid)

Three-fourths of Americans say it's inevitable that marijuana will be legal for recreational use across the nation, whether they support such policies or not, according to a public opinion poll released Wednesday that highlights shifting attitudes following the drug war era and tough-on-crime legislation.

The Pew Research Center survey also shows increased support for ending mandatory minimum prison sentences for non-violent drug offenders and doing away altogether with jail time for small amounts of marijuana. The opinions come as public debate on these topics has led lawmakers around the nation to consider policy changes. Since California became the first state to legalize medical marijuana in 1996, at least 19 others and the District of Columbia have followed suit, including two that have approved recreational use. More than a dozen state legislatures considered legalization measures this year.

Meanwhile, critics and political leaders, both liberal and conservative, have clamored for an end to harsh drug sentences, saying mandatory minimums have contributed to prison overcrowding, civil rights violations and strained budgets. U.S. Attorney General Eric Holder has been pushing Congress to overhaul drug sentencing policies. The telephone survey found that 75 percent of respondents — including majorities of both supporters and opponents of legal marijuana — think that the sale and use of pot eventually will be legal nationwide.

It was the first time that question had been asked, but it reflects a gradual trend of acceptance. The survey indicates that four years ago, 52 percent of respondents said they thought the use of marijuana should not be legal, while 41 percent said it should. The new poll shows a reversal with 54 percent in favor of legalization and 42 percent opposed. It marked a turning point in a gap that has been shrinking fairly steadily since 1969, the earliest data available, when 84 percent said pot should be illegal and only 12 percent thought otherwise. "Pot just doesn't seem as bad," said Gregory Carlson, a 52-year-old landscaper from Denver who did not participate in the Pew survey. "You don't see anything about someone smoking a joint and then driving the wrong way into a school bus," Carlson said.

With a chuckle, he added Wednesday, April 2, 2014, "They just drive slower." The survey also highlighted a dramatic shift in attitudes on drug conviction penalties. The survey was about evenly divided in 2001 on whether it was good or bad for states to move away from mandatory minimum sentences for non-violent drug offenders. Today, poll respondents favored moving away from such policies by a nearly 2-to-1 margin, or 63 percent to 32 percent. Respondents said by a margin greater than 3-to-1 that people who use small amounts of pot shouldn't go to jail. "Even people who don't favor the legalization of marijuana think the possession of small amounts shouldn't result in jail time," said Carroll Doherty, Pew's Director of Political Research. The nation thought differently a generation ago.

Congress passed the Anti-Drug Abuse Act in 1986 to set mandatory minimum sentences for federal drug crimes that could end up in life sentences for repeat offenders. Years later, many states reported prisons bursting at the seams, prompting public officials to start abandoning "lock 'em up" drug policies in the 1990s. The trend has since accelerated. Last month, Holder testified in support of proposed sentence reductions in an effort to reserve the "the harshest penalties for the most serious drug offenders." Such plans, including one drafted by Kentucky Republican Sen. Rand Paul, that would give judges wider discretion in sentencing have picked up support from both Republicans and Democrats.

The poll suggested that, despite shifting attitudes on legalization, the public remains concerned about drug abuse, with 32 percent of those surveyed calling it a crisis and 55 percent of respondents viewing it as a serious national problem. And a narrow majority, 54 percent, said marijuana legalization would lead to more underage people trying it. Marijuana legalization opponents, however, said the public isn't sold yet on legal pot. Kevin Sabet, cofounder of Smart Approaches to Marijuana, which opposes pot legalization, pointed to the fact that 63 percent said it would bother them if people used marijuana openly in their neighborhood. "Saying that we don't want people to serve prison time for marijuana is very different from saying I want a pot shop in my neighborhood selling cookies and candies and putting coupons in the paper," Sabet said.

The poll of 1,821 adults was conducted Feb. 14-23. The survey had a margin of error of plus or minus 2.6 percentage points.

Marijuana Needs Debate
November 25, 2014
By Susan Montoya Bryan

The conversation about whether New Mexico should join other Western states in legalizing marijuana is cranking up as state lawmakers prepare for the 2015 legislative session.

Rep. Bill McCamley, a Democrat from southern New Mexico, took his case for legalization to fellow lawmakers Tuesday, November 25, 2014 during a meeting of the interim health and human services committee.

McCamley dismissed the stoner humor of 1970s comics Cheech and Chong and said this should be a serious debate.

"Let's talk about the facts," he told the committee. "Let's talk about what's actually happening in terms of public policy, and let's not get caught up in stereotypes about what this is or isn't."

McCamley has yet to craft the legislation, but he's looking at Oregon as a model. Voters in that state, Alaska and the District of Columbia approved ballot initiatives to legalize marijuana earlier this month, joining Colorado and Washington.

In New Mexico, the push for legalization follows the success of ballot questions in two of the state's most populous counties that gauged voter support for decriminalizing marijuana.

"If you look at prohibition, it's basically a failure both in terms of alcohol in the 1920s and the drug war now," McCamley said during an interview. "We're spending all of this money enforcing marijuana laws and prosecuting people for smoking marijuana. That can be used in other law-enforcement efforts like prosecuting rapists and murderers — and that's important."

Then there's the potential for tax revenue.

There have been no studies on the economic effects legalization would have on New Mexico, a poor state and one that has long struggled when it comes to economic development. In neighboring Colorado, the state has brought in more than $52 million in taxes, licenses and fees for recreational and medical marijuana since the beginning of the year.

McCamley also estimates that the state could save over $33 million in costs associated with police, courts and corrections if marijuana is legalized.

"If we legalize and regulate marijuana, we get the benefits of the tax money. And the cartels that are creating a lot of violence both in the United States and internationally, we cut them off at the knees at the same time," he said.

A bill that would have let voters decide the issue failed during the last legislative session amid concerns about running afoul of federal law and possibly losing grant money from the U.S. Justice Department and other agencies for efforts to reduce drug trafficking and drug production.

The New Mexico Sheriffs' Association has yet to develop a position on the matter.

"Right now, there are several sheriffs who are very opposed to it.

We also have sheriffs who say let's wait and see and others who want it researched," said Jack LeVick, the group's executive director. "Before we jump on board as another state doing it, everybody needs to spend the time and really research the patterns and the problems that are existing."

Gov. Susana Martinez has been an outspoken critic of decriminalizing marijuana, and control of the state House of Representatives swinging to Republicans will likely make for a challenge in getting legislation passed.

"We don't want to get people's expectations up, but it's very important to have this conversation," McCamley said.

Adam Eidinger, chairman of the DC Cannabis Campaign, works on posters encouraging people to vote yes on DC Ballot Initiative 71 to legalize small amounts of marijuana for personal use, in Washington, October 9, 2014. (AP Photo/Jacquelyn Martin)

Rand Paul's College Days
December 6, 2014
By Kim Chandler

Kentucky Sen. Rand Paul hinted in an interview Friday December 5, 2014 that he smoked marijuana in his youth, adding that voters should not confuse his push for reduced criminal penalties for drug offenses as an endorsement of drug use.

Paul, who announced plans this week to seek re-election to the Senate in 2016 and is actively exploring whether to run for president, said he "wasn't a choir boy" when asked by Louisville television station WHAS if he had used marijuana while in college. "Let's just say I wasn't a choir boy when I was in college and that I can recognize that kids make mistakes, and I can say that I made mistakes when I was a kid," Paul said in an interview broadcast Friday night. "I think drugs, marijuana included, aren't good for you," Paul said. "I don't want to be someone who is seen as being this person advocating for drug use. I think they're not a good idea." The recreational use of marijuana is legal in two states and voters in two more plus the District of Columbia have approved legalization as well.

Paul told a group of law students at Northern Kentucky University last month he would not support lifting the federal ban on marijuana use, but said he did not want the federal government to try and overturn state laws that have made the drug legal. Paul told WHAS he has focused on reducing criminal penalties for some nonviolent drug offenses, which he said have been administered unfairly and disproportionally impact the nation's minorities.

He noted that the past three presidents "either admitted or skirted around the issue" of using illegal drugs in their youth. "If they had been poor or lived in poverty or lived in one of our big cities where there are a lot of (police) patrols, there's a good chance none of them would have ever excelled," Paul said. "So I have a great deal of personal sympathy for people who have made mistakes as a young person." Paul said in the interview a decision on whether to run for president was still months away.

However, he said any potential presidential campaign would include Jesse Benton, his 2010 Senate campaign manager, who resigned from Sen. Mitch McConnell's re-election campaign earlier this year after an Iowa state senator pleaded guilty to federal charges stemming from Paul's father's 2012 presidential campaign. Benton, who served as former Rep. Ron Paul's campaign manager in 2012, has denied any wrongdoing and has not been charged. In that case, former Iowa state Sen.

Kent Sorensen allegedly accepted thousands of dollars to switch his support to Ron Paul before the 2012 Iowa caucuses and lied to federal investigators about the money. "Jesse is married to my niece and was a big help in the Kentucky election here in 2010 and a big help for Sen. McConnell. Yes, he'll help us," Rand Paul said, adding he did not think Benton "did anything wrong."

What Teens Think
December 19, 2012
By Hope Yen

Teenagers' perception of the dangers of marijuana has fallen to the lowest level in more than 20 years, a new study (from November of 2012) says, prompting federal researchers to warn that already high use of the drug could increase as more states move to legalize it.

The annual survey released Wednesday by the National Institutes of Health found that only 41.7 percent of eighth graders believe that occasional use of marijuana is harmful, while 66.9 percent regard it as dangerous when used regularly. Both rates are the lowest since 1991, when the government first began tracking this age group.

Teens' perception of marijuana risks diminished even more as they got older. About 20.6 percent of 12th graders said that occasional use of pot is harmful. Roughly 44.1 percent believed that its regular use was detrimental, the lowest rate since 1979. The government-sponsored study said teens' dwindling concerns about the dangers of marijuana, despite the risks, "can signal future increases in use." "We are increasingly concerned that regular or daily use of marijuana is robbing many young people of their potential to achieve and excel in school or other aspects of life," said Dr. Nora D. Volkow, director of the National Institute on Drug Abuse, which is part of NIH.

She said teens are influenced by whether a drug is legal in some form when deciding to try it recreationally, so in states where marijuana is sanctioned, "the deterrent is no longer present." Volkow cited recently published research showing that people who used marijuana heavily before age 18 had impaired mental abilities even after they quit using the drug. Those who used cannabis heavily in their teens and into their adulthood showed a significant drop in IQ between the ages of 13 and 38, according to the studies. "Marijuana use that begins in adolescence increases the risk they will become addicted to the drug," she said.

The findings come after Washington state and Colorado voted to legalize marijuana and regulate its recreational use, boosted by the strong support of younger voters. While the new laws apply only to adults over 21, the broader effort by states to decriminalize pot use and push the drug toward public legitimacy could confuse the picture for teens. President Barack Obama said last week that the federal government won't go after pot users in Colorado and Washington state who are legal under their state laws, even though federal law officially bans marijuana possession.

Eighteen states and the District of Columbia also have laws in place to regulate the medical use of marijuana. "Now more than ever we need parents and other adult influencers to step up and have direct conversations with young people about the importance of making healthy decisions," said White House drug czar Gil Kerlikowske on Wednesday. According to the federal survey, marijuana use among teenagers remained stuck at high levels in 2012. Roughly 6.5 percent of 12th graders smoked marijuana daily, up from 5.1 percent in 2007.

Nearly 23 percent of the high-school seniors said they smoked the drug in the month prior to the survey, while 36.4 percent used it in the past year. About 45.2 percent reported they had tried marijuana at least once in their lifetime. Daily marijuana use by 10th graders climbed from 2.8 percent to 3.5 percent, and for eighth-grade students it edged up from 0.8 percent to 1.1 percent.

On other topics the survey found: —Use of illicit drugs other than marijuana was at a low for eighth-, 10th- and 12th-grade students. —In the past year, about 1.3 percent of 12th graders used "bath salts," a new synthetic drug which mimics the effect of cocaine. —In terms of prescription drug abuse, about 7.6 percent of 12th graders in the past year used Adderall, a stimulant prescribed to treat ADHD. That's up from 5.4 percent in 2009, coinciding with a decline in teens' perceptions of the harm in using the drug.

Teen abuse of over-the-counter cough and cold medicines containing dextromethorphan held steady. —Reported alcohol use continued to steadily decline, falling to the lowest level on record. The survey, conducted by the University of Michigan for NIH, covered more than 45,000 students in the eighth, 10th and 12th grades in 395 schools.

Marijuana in Latin America
October 29, 2014
By The Associated Press

Here's a look at the status of marijuana laws in some countries in Latin America and the Caribbean.

ARGENTINA:

Personal possession of marijuana was decriminalized under a 2009 Supreme Court ruling that jail time for small amounts of drugs violates Argentina's constitution. Although the ruling only referred to pot, in practice it extended to most drugs.

BRAZIL:

Does not punish personal drug use, but trafficking or transporting small amounts of controlled substances is punishable by drug abuse education or community service.

CHILE:

The law allows use of medical marijuana, but so far only one pilot program has been authorized. First legal seeds were planted Wednesday.

COLOMBIA:

President Juan Manuel Santos in August endorsed newly introduced legislation that would legalize marijuana for medicinal and therapeutic use in the drug war-afflicted Andean nation.

GUATEMALA:

President Otto Perez Molina has called the drug war a failed strategy and praised the "visionary" legalization experiments in Washington and Colorado. Currently, prison terms of four months to two years can be imposed for the possession of drugs for personal use.

JAMAICA:

The justice minister in June announced legislation to decriminalize the possession of to 2 ounces (57 grams) of pot and legalize the drug for religious purposes in a country where adherents of the Rastafarian spiritual movement ritually smoke marijuana as a "holy herb."

MEXICO:

There is no general push to legalize marijuana in a country where tens of thousands have been killed in drug war violence in the past seven years, but lawmakers in the capital, Mexico City, have introduced a measure to allow stores to sell up to 5 grams of pot.

URUGUAY:

Became the first nation to approve a state-overseen marijuana market in 2013. Once registered and licensed, any Uruguayan adult will be allowed to grow plants at home or join a pot-growing club. Soon users will also be able to buy marijuana cigarettes from pharmacies.

7

At the Ballot Box

Marijuana in the 2014 Elections
November 5, 2014
By David Crary

Voters in Oregon and the District of Columbia legalized the use of recreational pot, elating marijuana activists who hope to extend their winning streak across the country. Oregon will join the company of Colorado and Washington state, where voters approved the recreational use of marijuana two years ago, since November of 2014.

The District of Columbia is on the same path unless Congress, which has review power, blocks the move. Another marijuana-legalization measure in Alaska was maintaining a steady lead in early returns. Other volatile issues on state ballots on Tuesday include gambling and abortion. Voters in Washington state, faced with two competing measures on gun sales, approved an expansion of background checks. And several states including Arkansas and South Dakota approved minimum wage increases. The District of Columbia's marijuana measure would make it legal to possess up to two ounces of pot and up to three mature marijuana plants for personal use, but it does not provide for the legal sale of marijuana, leaving that matter up to the D.C. Council.

That's different from the measures in Oregon and Alaska, which would follow the example of Colorado and Washington state in setting up systems for regulating and taxing retail sales of marijuana. The Drug Policy Alliance, one of the leaders of the legalization campaign, said Tuesday's results would bolster its efforts to push through a ballot measure in California in 2016. "The pace of reform is accelerating, other states are sure to follow, and even Congress is poised to wake from its slumber," said Ethan Nadelmann, the alliance's executive director.

Oregon's measure calls for pot legalization by July 1, and requires the state Liquor Control Commission to adopt regulations by Jan. 1, 2016. The state's sheriffs were among the law's chief opponents, contending that legalization would give children access to marijuana and could lead to more people driving under the influence. The campaign in D.C. included a debate about race — the measure's supporters said blacks in the city had been disproportionately targeted for marijuana arrests. "The criminal justice system is getting bogged down by marijuana use, and a lot of the people who use marijuana aren't criminals," said Gary Fulwood, a support staffer for the city's fire and EMS department who voted for the initiative. "I don't see it being any worse than alcohol." In Florida, a measure that would have allowed marijuana use for medical reasons fell short of the 60 percent approval to pass; near-complete returns showed it getting about 57 percent of the vote. Twenty-three states allow medical marijuana.

Congress to Weigh In
November 5, 2014
By Ben Nuckols

The national marijuana legalization debate is moving into the backyard of a Republican-controlled Congress, now that the District of Columbia has voted to legalize growing, possessing and sharing small amounts of pot. Voters in Oregon and Alaska also approved legalization initiatives, joining Colorado and Washington state, where pot is already legally available.

But while states out West enjoy both autonomy and distance, federal lawmakers have the power to quash any District law they don't like. And with legalization getting a foothold on the East Coast for the first time, the District's initiative could force Congress to make decisions affecting the future of legal pot nationwide. "Members of Congress are literally going to be witness to these changes," said Ethan Nadelmann, executive director of the Drug Policy Alliance, which spent heavily to push all three ballot initiatives. "It's a form of educating the members of Congress in a way that some members would not get educated, depending on the states that they're from."

All laws in the nation's capital are sent to Capitol Hill for review. Congress rarely invokes that power, but when members do want to block District policies, they can attach amendments to unrelated, omnibus legislation too critical to be vetoed. Congress routinely bars the spending of local tax dollars on abortions for poor women using this strategy, and delayed medical marijuana in the District for more than a decade.

The District voted 69-31 percent Tuesday to approve the growing, possessing or sharing of up to two ounces of pot and up to three mature marijuana plants for personal use. Months earlier, a decriminalization law took effect, limiting the penalty for possession of a personal-use amount to a $25 ticket. But it could take months at least before pot-smoking is totally OK in the District.

Elected officials and advocates can't even agree whether the Congressional review period lasts 30 days while the House and Senate are both in session, or 60. Also, the initiative doesn't provide for the legal sale or taxation of marijuana. Democratic mayor-elect Muriel Bowser said Wednesday that she won't let it take effect until the D.C. Council implements rules that she said could be "similar to how we tax and regulate alcohol." D.C. Cannabis Campaign chairman Adam Eidinger vowed to challenge any delay, which he said could thwart the will of the voters for years. Colorado allowed home cultivation for more than a year before its first marijuana dispensaries opened, he noted. "Three plants or less doesn't need to be taxed and regulated," he said. "They don't regulate people who brew their own beer."

The incoming mayor has no immediate power over the initiative but once she takes office in January she could introduce a bill that delays implementation until a regulatory scheme is enacted.

Rep. Andy Harris, a Maryland Republican, tried to block the decriminalization law, and said Wednesday that he'll try to block legalization as well, arguing that drug use among teenagers will rise if they fail to stop it. But polls have shown a majority of Americans favor legalization, and Republicans are far from united in opposition. Sen. Rand Paul of Kentucky, the ranking Republican on the subcommittee that oversees the District, said Tuesday that the city's pot laws should be left to local officials. Paul also has sought to block the federal government from interfering with states' medical marijuana programs.

If the Republican-led Congress does try to quash the initiative by amending some bill President Barack Obama won't veto, it could force him antagonize his base after advocates pointed to the huge racial disparities in marijuana arrests in the nation's capital. In Florida, 58 percent of voters were for legalization of medical marijuana on Tuesday, November 5 2014, narrowly missing the 60 percent needed to amend the state's constitution. "This is just the first battle, and I plan to win the war," said Orlando trial attorney John Morgan, who vowed Wednesday to begin working on another try in 2016.

Other legalization advocates plan a big push for similar initiatives on 2016 ballots in California, Arizona, Maine, Massachusetts and Nevada, Nadelmann said. Legalization opponent Kevin Sabet, the president of Smart Approaches to Marijuana, said his side would need to respond in kind. Tuesday's votes were "a bit of a wake-up call before 2016," he said, noting that legalization advocates had vastly outspent opponents this time.

8

The NFL

Right Answers for Marijuana Use
August 14, 2014
By Eddie Pells

Seattle Seahawks NFL football head coach Pete Carroll talks to the media during a news conference in Renton, Wash. As attitudes toward marijuana use soften, and science slowly teases out marijuana's possible benefits for concussions and other injuries, the NFL is reaching a critical point in navigating its tenuous relationship with what is being recognized, more and more, as the analgesic of choice for many of its players. At least one high-profile coach, Pete Carroll of the Seahawks, said he'd like to see the NFL study whether marijuana can help players, April 4, 2014. (AP Photo/Marcus R. Donner, File)

Marijuana is casting an ever-thickening haze across NFL locker rooms, and it's not simply because more players are using it. As attitudes toward the drug soften, and science slowly teases out marijuana's possible benefits for concussions and other injuries, the NFL is reaching a critical point in navigating its tenuous relationship with what is recognized as the analgesic of choice for many of its players. "It's not, let's go smoke a joint," retired NFL defensive lineman Marvin Washington said. "It's, what if you could take something that helps you heal faster from a concussion, that prevents your equilibrium from being off for two weeks and your eyesight for being off for four weeks?"

One challenge the NFL faces is how to bring marijuana into the game as a pain reliever without condoning its use as a recreational drug. And facing a lawsuit filed on behalf of hundreds of former players complaining about the effects of prescription painkillers they say were pushed on them by team trainers and doctors, the NFL is looking for other ways to help players deal with the pain from a violent game. A Gallup poll last year found 58 percent of Americans believe marijuana should be legalized. That's already happened in Colorado and Washington — the states that are home of last season's Super Bowl teams.

The World Anti-Doping Agency has said it does not need to catch out-of-competition marijuana users. And at least one high-profile coach, Pete Carroll of the champion Seahawks, publicly said he'd like to see the NFL study whether marijuana can help players. There are no hard numbers on how many NFL players are using marijuana, but anecdotal evidence, including the arrest or league discipline of no fewer than a dozen players for pot over the past 18 months, suggests use is becoming more common. Washington Redskins defensive back Ryan Clark didn't want to pinpoint the number of current NFL players who smoke pot but said, "I know a lot of guys who don't regularly smoke marijuana who would use it during the season."

Washington wouldn't put a specific number on it but said he, too, knew his share of players who weren't shy about lighting up when he was in the league, including one guy "who just hated the pain pills they were giving out at the time." Another longtime defensive lineman, Marcellus Wiley, estimates half the players in the average NFL locker room were using it by the time he shut down his career in 2006. "They are leaning on it to cope with the pain," said Wiley, who played defensive line in the league for 10 seasons. "They are leaning on it to cope with the anxiety of the game."

The NFL is fighting lawsuits on two fronts — concussions and painkillers — both of which, some argue, could be positively influenced if marijuana were better tolerated by the league. The science, however, is slow-moving and expensive and might not ever be conclusive, says behavioral psychologist Ryan Vandrey, who studies marijuana use at John Hopkins.

Marijuana may work better for some people, while narcotics and other painkillers might be better for others. "Different medicines work differently from person to person," Vandrey said. "There's pretty good science that shows marijuana does have pain relieving properties. Whether it's a better pain reliever than the other things available has never been evaluated."

Washington, who is part of the concussion lawsuit, is working with a biopharmaceutical and phyto-medical company called KannaLife Sciences that recently received licensing from the National Institutes of Health (NIH) to develop a drug to treat concussions using derivatives from medical marijuana.

Co-founder Thoma Kikis, who has been working on cannibas-based solutions to concussions for a few years, said he approached the NFL about signing on to the research. "They didn't want to meet, didn't want to take a position to create any kind of controversy," Kikis said. "I understand that. But ultimately, they're going to have to make a decision and look into different research." NFL Commissioner Roger Goodell has treaded gingerly around the subject. Before last season's Super Bowl he said the league would "follow the medicine" and not rule out allowing players to use marijuana for medical purposes.

An NFL spokesman reiterated that this month, saying if medical advisers inform the league it should consider modifying the policy, it would explore possible changes. A spokesman for the players union declined comment on marijuana, beyond saying the union is always looking for ways to improve the drug-testing policy.

But earlier this year, NFLPA executive director DeMaurice Smith said the marijuana policy is secondary when set against the failure to bring Human Growth Hormone testing into the game. Some believe relaxing the marijuana rules could be linked to a deal that would bring in HGH testing. "I've heard that in conversations," said Wiley, a plaintiff in the painkiller lawsuit. "And I think it's despicable that you'd pit them against each other."

The NFL drug policy has come under even more scrutiny this summer, after the NFL handed down a season-long suspension of Browns receiver Josh Gordon for multiple violations of the NFL substance-abuse policy.

That suspension, especially when juxtaposed against the two-game ban Ray Rice received for domestic violence, has led some to say the league's priorities are out of whack. In June, Harvard Medical School professor emeritus Lester Grinspoon, one of the forefathers of marijuana research, published an open letter to Goodell, urging him to drop urine testing for weed altogether and, more importantly, fund a crash research project for a marijuana-based drug that can alleviate the consequences of concussions.

"As much as I love to watch professional football, I'm beginning to feel like a Roman in the days when they would send Christians to the lions," Grinspoon said. "I don't want to be part of an audience that sees kids ruin their future with this game, and then the league doesn't give them any recourse to try to protect themselves." The league does fund sports-health research at the NIH to the tune of a $30 million donation it made in 2012.

But the science moves slowly no matter where it's conducted and, as Vandrey says, "the NFL is in business for playing football, not doing scientific research." Meanwhile, marijuana becomes more and more acceptable across America every day. But even with the Super Bowl being dubbed "The Stoner Bowl" and the issue hanging heavily over the NFL's marquee event, the league has shown no signs of quick movement.

New Drug Policy Proposed
September 9, 2014
By Barry Wilner

Mason Tvert, right, spokesman for the Marijuana Policy Project, prepares to deliver a petition to National Football League headquarters in New York. Kevin Fitzgerald, left, director of building security, waits for the handoff. Tvert's organization is asking the NFL to allow its players to use marijuana in states where it is legal to do so. Both Washington and Colorado have legalized marijuana use, January 29, 2014. (AP Photo/Mark Lennihan)

The league's threshold for a positive test remains 10 times lower than that of WADA, which changed its limit last year in a nod to the reality that the drug is not a performance enhancer. The NFL's conundrum is figuring a graceful way to keep tabs on those who use marijuana recklessly — or recreationally — while giving others a legitimate form of pain relief. "I'd like to see us advance the subject to where we're all mature and we get it," Wiley said, "and we let players make the decision for themselves."

The 32 player representatives to the union have delayed a vote on the NFL's proposal for changes to the drug policy that potentially could implement HGH testing. After a conference call of about one hour on the night of Tuesday September 9, 2014, during which the proposal was discussed, the player reps opted to take no action.

The proposal was not delivered to the union until midday. "There was no vote tonight by NFLPA player representatives," Union spokesman George Atallah said. "We will continue to work towards a comprehensive agreement." The union has insisted that a satisfactory proposal to them is the only one that will be voted on.

Atallah said last week that a "piecemeal" agreement did not interest the players. The sides have discussed changes to the policy on substance abuse and driving under the influence of drugs/alcohol.

A potential hang-up on that issue was the league's desire to immediately discipline players — as well as NFL owners, executives, officials, coaches and league office personnel — arrested for DUIs. NFLPA President Eric Winston told The Associated Press last week that ignoring a player's rights to due process would not be considered by the union.

The NFLPA also is pushing for neutral arbitration in the appeals process and is seeking higher thresholds for positive marijuana tests. But the key element could be a test for human growth hormone. HGH testing was agreed upon in the 2011 collective bargaining agreement that ended the lockout of the players. But the union has been uncomfortable with the science and the procedures for the testing, as well as how appeals would be handled.

The league did agree to an appeal process several years ago.

In marijuana testing, the union feels the league's threshold for a positive test of 15 nanograms per milliliter is too demanding, citing the IOC's threshold of 150 nanograms, 10 times as high. The NFL threshold was collectively bargained.

But as Winston said last Friday, anyone within the vicinity of people smoking marijuana without partaking themselves could wind up testing positive at such a low number. "The (potency) level is so much greater in marijuana now, the secondhand smoke can get a positive test," Winston said.

"Just a guy who is around it second hand, then to have to go into the program? We don't want false positive. We have to move up the minimum to normal workplace standards."

HGH Testing Debated
September 13, 2014
By Barry Wilner

Hours after the players' union voted Friday September 12, 2014 to accept an NFL proposal on drug policy changes that included HGH testing, the league says it is not a done deal.

Player representatives to the union also voted for changes to marijuana testing, classification for amphetamines, punishment for driving under the influence, and neutral arbitration on appeals. But NFL spokesman Greg Aiello said Friday in an email to The Associated Press: "There are unresolved issues. More negotiation ahead."

Aiello did not specify which issues are not resolved, but called them "significant." Testing for human growth hormone was originally agreed upon in 2011, but the players have balked at the science in the testing and the appeals process for positive tests. If the proposal they voted on Friday is put into action, testing would begin for this season.

The player reps also approved an increase for the threshold for positive marijuana tests. Some players have complained that the NFL threshold of 15 nanograms per milliliter is so low that anyone within the vicinity of people smoking marijuana could test positive. The threshold was increased to 35 ng/ml in the league's proposal. On Saturday, the NFL Players Association issued a statement: "We hope to have final agreements, including effective date for players with adjusted discipline, very soon." Overall changes are retroactive for players suspended under previous policies, as well as for those in the appeal process.

Those players, including Browns receiver Josh Gordon (suspended for the season) and Broncos receiver Wes Welker (four games), are subject to standards of the new policies. Their suspensions could be reduced. However, no immediate announcements were made regarding those suspensions, probably because the NFL doesn't consider anything official yet. Welker was suspended for amphetamine use in the offseason, but punishment for that is being switched from the performance enhancers policy to the substance abuse program — except for in-season violations. A two-game suspension would be issued for a player convicted of driving under the influence. But an NFL proposal to immediately suspend a player, owner, coach, team executive or league employee for a DUI arrest was rejected by the union. The players approved arbitration for appeals under the substance abuse and the PED policies.

The NFL and NFL Players Association would hire between three and five arbitrators. The league and the union also would retain independent investigators to review cases in which player confidentiality under the drug policy had been breached. Punishment for leaks could range up to $500,000 and/or termination of a job. "This is an historic moment for our players and our league," NFLPA President Eric Winston said before the NFL basically put matters on hold. "We have collectively bargained drug policies that will keep the game clean and safe, but also provide our players with an unprecedented level of fairness and transparency."

1st Offender Program
December 3, 2014
By Joe Mandak

Pittsburgh Steelers running back Le'Veon Bell has applied for a first-offender's program on marijuana possession and driving under the influence charges, which could result in the charges being dismissed and his arrest record expunged, his attorney said Wednesday December 3, 2014.

The tentative deal would include 15 months of probation and a 60-day driver's license suspension, attorney Robert Del Greco Jr. said. It must be approved by an Allegheny County judge Feb. 6.

Bell would also owe roughly $2,000 in court costs, which include fees to participate in the first-offender's program and a drunken driving school. Bell must also have a drug and alcohol evaluation, participate in driving under the influence group therapy and undergo a court-ordered assessment and follow any treatment recommendations, Del Greco said.

Under the program, Bell does not have to plead guilty. Instead, once the judge confirms he's eligible for the program, Bell will begin serving his probation and can ask the court to clear his record if he completes the other terms without incident.

Del Greco spelled out the agreement when Bell was formally arraigned on the charges Wednesday in county court. Bell was in court but didn't comment. Bell and fellow Steelers running back LeGarrette Blount were arrested Aug. 20 after a motorcycle officer in suburban Ross Township reported smelling marijuana coming from a vehicle they were in with a female companion.

Blount was cut after he left the field early following a loss to the Tennessee Titans last month and now plays for New England. He faces a preliminary hearing Dec. 10. Bell is the Steelers' leading rusher with 1,046 yards on 218 carries and is second in the league to the Dallas Cowboy's DeMarco Murray, who has rushed for 1,427 yards. Bell has also caught 65 passes for 643 yards.

Del Greco said Bell is being tested for drugs weekly under NFL rules and will likely face a two-game NFL suspension once the criminal case wraps up.

Del Greco said Pennsylvania has a "zero tolerance" standard for driving under the influence of illegal drugs like marijuana, and a hospital blood test showed Bell had marijuana in his system after he was pulled over even though he told police he was "perfectly fine" and not impaired. Police seized about 20 grams — or three-fourths of an ounce — of marijuana in a plastic bag found in the car's console.

New England Patriots running back LeGarrette Blount, center, leaves a district court with his attorney, Casey White, in West View, Pa. after a preliminary hearing on a marijuana possession charge stemming from an August traffic stop when he was with the Pittsburgh Steelers. The judge said he'll dismiss the marijuana possession charge against Blount if he completes 50 hours of community service by a Feb. 4 court date. Steelers running back Le'Veon Bell was driving the car and also charged, December 10, 2014. (AP Photo/Keith Srakocic)

MARIJUANA-RELATED INCIDENTS IN THE NFL | 2013 - 2014

- Josh Gordon reinstated | Sept. 19, 2014
- NFL, union agree to new drug policy | Sept. 17, 2014
- Suspension for Browns Gordon | Aug. 27, 2014
- Should NFL to fund medical marijuana studies? | June 16, 2014
- Former Giants Hill violates drug policy | May 30, 2014
- Cardinals Washington one-year suspension | May 30, 2014
- Director of NFLPA critical of Goodell | May 29, 2014
- Bills Dareus arrested for synthetic marijuana | May 5, 2014
- Seahawks Browner third-time offender | Feb. 2, 2014
- Goodell doesn't rule out medical marijuana | Jan. 23, 2014
- HBO reports use among players | Jan. 21, 2014
  The 'Stoner Bowl' | Jan. 19, 2014
- Jaguars Blackmon suspended indefinitely | Nov. 1, 2013
- Broncos Miller suspension | Aug. 20, 2013

9

The Future

Who Goes Legal Next?
November 23, 2014
By Patrick Whittle

State Rep. Allen Peake, R-Macon, left, embraces Janea Cox after a bill Peake sponsored that would legalize medical marijuana in Georgia for patients with certain illnesses like Cox's daughter passed on the House floor, in Atlanta, March 3, 2014. (AP Photo/David Goldman)

Marijuana advocates want to finally take their legalization drive — thus far the province of western states — to the Northeast, and they say the first state to do it here might be Maine.

The Pine Tree State has a long history with cannabis — Maine voters approved medical marijuana legalization 15 years ago, becoming the first state to do so in New England. Now, national marijuana advocates say, the state represents a chance for pro-marijuana forces to get a toe-hold in the northeastern states they have long coveted. Supporters of marijuana legalization say part of their focus on Maine is schematic — the ease of Maine's citizen-led public ballot initiative process makes it a more viable target than states where laws can only be changed through complicated state legislative battles.

Pro-legalization advocates also cite a pair of recent victories in municipal legalization drives — Portland, the state's largest city, in 2013 and South Portland, its fourth largest, this month. Maine also decriminalized the possession of small amounts of marijuana nearly four decades ago, and the state already has a sizeable network of eight dispensaries and more than 1,500 legal growers.

The favorable climate for legalization has national and local pro-marijuana groups gearing up for a potential statewide legalization ballot initiative in 2016. "It's quite possible that Maine could be the first state in the Northeast to legalize marijuana and other states would follow," said Bill Piper, director of national affairs for the Washington, D.C.-based Drug Policy Alliance.

Marijuana reformers around the country scored a series of wins on election night, when Oregon, Alaska and Washington, D.C., all went legal. Maine supporters are already crafting the ballot initiative for the 2016 election cycle, according to David Boyer, a Falmouth resident and political director for the Washington-based Marijuana Policy Project. The petitioners will need to collect about 61,000 signatures to get the item on the ballot, according to the state constitution. Boyer said the petition drive will likely begin in the next six months.

Maine does have some competition to be first to legalize in the Northeast, as national advocates are also targeting Massachusetts for a potential referendum in 2016. State legislatures in Rhode Island and Vermont could also take up the issue next year. Outside the Northeast, national advocates are also pushing for popular ballot initiatives in California, Arizona and Nevada. Maine's ballot initiative will face significant opposition from some public and law enforcement officials, some of whom campaigned against legalization in its cities.

Some medical marijuana advocates also have reservations, including Hillary Lister, director of the Medical Marijuana Caregivers of Maine, who said she fears large-scale investors could crowd smaller growers out of the market. Roy McKinney, director of the Maine Drug Enforcement Agency, said the legalization vote in South Portland — where voters approved a measure to allow people age 21 and older to possess an ounce of marijuana — doesn't supersede state law.

He said the agency's stance on the statewide ballot initiative would depend on how it was written, but added that it opposed efforts to legalize marijuana via the state legislature. Approval on a statewide level won't sail through, as anti-marijuana forces are emboldened by a recent victory of their own — a November legalization referendum's failure in Lewiston, the state's second-largest city.

Lewiston Mayor Bob Macdonald, who worked in the drug unit of Lewiston's police department before becoming mayor, called legalization a sign of "degeneration of society." He said he is glad the referendum to legalize marijuana in his city failed. "I'm set in my ways and that's one thing I'm totally against — making any drugs legal," he said.

Lindsey Kelly works at the campaign office for the Yes on CC measure in Santa Ana, Calif. Measure CC regulates and controls medical cannabis dispensaries in the city of Santa Ana, October 23, 2014. (AP Photo/Chris Carlson)

A U.S. private equity firm announced Tuesday it has joined the family of late reggae star Bob Marley in hopes of building what it touts as the "world's first global cannabis brand."

Seattle-based Privateer Holdings announced Tuesday it has reached a licensing deal with Marley's heirs to offer marijuana strains, including ones famed in Jamaica, where regulations permit by late 2015. It also plans to sell weed-infused lotions, creams and various accessories. "My dad would be so happy to see people understanding the healing power of the herb," Miami-based Cedella Marley said in a company statement. She's the eldest daughter of the music legend who died of cancer in 1981 and is Jamaica's most iconic figure.

Over the years, his estate has authorized deals for a wide range of merchandise. But the move to create "Marley Natural" has stirred grousing in Jamaica among those who share his Rastafarian faith, a spiritual movement that considers the drug divine.

Maxine Stowe of the Rastafari Millennium Council asserts that Marley was "the least of the Wailers around the issue of ganja legalization" and worries his estate's efforts to launch a cannabis brand will negatively impact future efforts in Jamaica to financially benefit from a legalization movement gaining traction across the globe.

Marijuana Marketing
November 18, 2014
By David McFadden

Yeni Sleidi, known as the "weed fairy," poses for a photo in Seattle's Capitol Hill neighborhood where this past weekend she posted 50 fliers with nuggets of marijuana taped to them. Sleidi, a 23-year-old who works in social media, has been visiting Seattle from New York where last year she did a similar posting, albeit anonymously, May 28, 2014. (AP Photo/Elaine Thompson)

A U.S. private equity firm announced Tuesday it has joined the family of late reggae star Bob Marley in hopes of building what it touts as the "world's first global cannabis brand."

Ashley Green trims a marijuana flower at the Pioneer Production and Processing marijuana growing facility in Arlington, Wash. Washington's second-in-the-nation legal marijuana market opened last summer to a dearth of weed, with some stores periodically closed because they didn't have pot to sell and prices were through the roof. Six months later, the equation has flipped, bringing serious growing pains to the new industry. Prices are starting to come down in the state's licensed pot shops, but due to a glut, growers are struggling to sell their marijuana, January 13, 2015. (AP Photo/Elaine Thompson)

Seattle-based Privateer Holdings announced Tuesday it has reached a licensing deal with Marley's heirs to offer marijuana strains, including ones famed in Jamaica, where regulations permit by late 2015. It also plans to sell weed-infused lotions, creams and various accessories.

"My dad would be so happy to see people understanding the healing power of the herb," Miami-based Cedella Marley said in a company statement. She's the eldest daughter of the music legend who died of cancer in 1981 and is Jamaica's most iconic figure.

Over the years, his estate has authorized deals for a wide range of merchandise. But the move to create "Marley Natural" has stirred grousing in Jamaica among those who share his Rastafarian faith, a spiritual movement that considers the drug divine.

Maxine Stowe of the Rastafari Millennium Council asserts that Marley was "the least of the Wailers around the issue of ganja legalization" and worries his estate's efforts to launch a cannabis brand will negatively impact future efforts in Jamaica to financially benefit from a legalization movement gaining traction across the globe.

Smaller-dose pot-infused cookies, called the Rookie Cookie, sit on the packaging table at The Growing Kitchen, in Boulder, September 26, 2014. (AP Photo/Brennan Linsley, File)

The Wailers were founded by Marley, Bunny Wailer and Peter Tosh. All three famously espoused smoking the "holy herb," but Stowe argues Wailer and the late Tosh were more strident activists.

"The government has to stand up now for Rastafari and the Wailers' rights in their intellectual property!" Stowe wrote in a Tuesday email.

Some Rastas are also irked that Marley Natural will be based in New York.

But pot remains prohibited here, even if Jamaica has been rethinking its position. The government hopes to amend drug laws to pave the way for a regulated medical marijuana and research sector. Officials say this could be achieved next year.

Delano Seiveright, director of the island's Ganja Law Reform Coalition, said there are hopes that the Marley family's plans will spur Jamaica to "develop a legal and regulated cannabis industry much sooner rather than later."

Pot for Moms in Colorado
February 3, 2015
By Kristen Wyatt

Marijuana use by pregnant or nursing women might seem like a no-brainer of a bad idea, but a proposal in Colorado to step up such warnings is raising concern because of limited or inconclusive research on the dangers.

Pot users in Colorado and Washington already receive warnings that the drug shouldn't be used by pregnant and nursing women. But a Colorado bill facing its first hearing Tuesday proposes going further by requiring pot shops to post signs saying that maternal marijuana use poses risks to unborn children.

"It's important to have notification that there is risk," said Republican Rep. Jack Tate, sponsor of the bill.

The proposal is controversial. Some pregnant women use marijuana to ease nausea, and a marijuana industry group fears the warnings don't acknowledge limited research on pot use by mothers-to-be.

Tyler Henson, president of the Colorado Cannabis Chamber of Commerce, called the proposal "another attempt to discredit and ignore the popular public opinion of marijuana's medicinal use."

A Colorado health report issued this week notes that marijuana's psychoactive ingredient, THC, is passed to children through the placenta and breast milk. But the doctors who compiled the survey of existing research also noted that the health consequences of that THC exposure aren't fully understood.

The report's authors found:

- "Mixed" evidence for pot's link to birth defects;
- "Insufficient" evidence that marijuana use during pregnancy makes offspring more likely to use pot themselves as adolescents;
- "Moderate" evidence that maternal use of marijuana during pregnancy is associated with attention problems, cognitive impairment or low IQ in offspring; and
- "Mixed" evidence that marijuana use during pregnancy is associated with low birth weight.

Still, the doctors concluded, "There is no known safe amount of marijuana use during pregnancy."

The report, released Monday, reflected national conclusions on marijuana's health risks.

Ali Maffey, retail marijuana education manager for the Colorado Department of Health and Environment, talks to reporters after a news conference to announce the rollout of the $5.7-million, state-sponsored advertising campaign. The "Good to Know" advertisements will focus on marijuana laws and health effects, including the ban on use in public places, age restrictions, DUI laws, the dangers of overuse and other concerns related to the use of the products. A legislative bill is facing its first hearing on Tuesday, Feb. 3, that proposes pot shops post signs warning of the risks that maternal marijuana use poses to unborn children, January 5, 2015. (AP Photo/David Zalubowski, File)

An American Academy of Pediatrics report in 2013 listed marijuana among the most common drugs involved in prenatal exposure that may pose important health risks, including possible behavior and attention problems in childhood.

The National Institute on Drug Abuse says animal studies have suggested that smoking marijuana in pregnancy may harm brain development. But the institute also says more research is needed "to disentangle marijuana's specific effects from other environmental factors, including maternal nutrition, exposure to nurturing/neglect, and use of other substances by mothers."

Colorado, one of four states that have legalized recreational use of pot, requires marijuana to carry labels saying, among other things, "There may be additional health risks associated with the consumption of this product for women who are pregnant, breastfeeding or planning on becoming pregnant."

In Washington state, marijuana purchasers are given warnings that include the statement, "Should not be used by women that are pregnant or breastfeeding."

Business Savvy

Struggling with Glut
January 16, 2015
By Gene Johnson

A pot store employee talks with customers inside the soon-to-move out Breckenridge Cannabis Club, which sells recreational marijuana products, in the ski town of Breckenridge, Colo. Business is booming in Colorado's mountain resorts, and the addition of recreational marijuana stores this year has attracted droves of customers curious about legalized pot. But in some quarters, there's anxiety that ski towns have embraced marijuana a little too much, December 11, 2014. (AP Photo/Brennan Linsley)

Washington's legal marijuana market opened in the summer of 2014 to a dearth of weed. Some stores periodically closed because they didn't have pot to sell. Prices were through the roof.

Six months later, the equation has flipped, bringing serious growing pains to the new industry.

A big harvest of sun-grown marijuana from eastern Washington last fall flooded the market. Prices are starting to come down in the state's licensed pot shops, but due to the glut, growers are - surprisingly - struggling to sell their marijuana. Some are already worried about going belly-up, finding it tougher than expected to make a living in legal weed.

"It's an economic nightmare," says Andrew Seitz, general manager at Dutch Brothers Farms in Seattle.

State data show that licensed growers had harvested 31,000 pounds of bud as of Thursday, January 16, 2015, but Washington's relatively few legal pot shops have sold less than one-fifth of that. Many of the state's marijuana users have stuck with the untaxed or much-lesser-taxed pot they get from black market dealers or unregulated medical dispensaries - limiting how quickly product moves off the shelves of legal stores.

"Every grower I know has got surplus inventory and they're concerned about it," said Scott Masengill, who has sold half of the 280 pounds he harvested from his pot farm in central Washington. "I don't know anybody getting rich."

Officials at the state Liquor Control Board, which regulates marijuana, aren't terribly concerned.

So far, there are about 270 licensed growers in Washington - but only about 85 open stores for them to sell to. That's partly due to a slow, difficult licensing process; retail applicants who haven't been ready to open; and pot business bans in many cities and counties.

The board's legal pot project manager, Randy Simmons, says he hopes about 100 more stores will open in the next few months, providing additional outlets for the weed that's been harvested.

Washington is always likely to have a glut of marijuana after the outdoor crop comes in each fall, he suggested, as the outdoor growers typically harvest one big crop which they continue to sell throughout the year.

Weed is still pricey at the state's pot shops - often in the $23-to-$25-per-gram range. That's about twice the cost at medical dispensaries, but cheaper than it was a few months ago.

Simmons said he expects pot prices to keep fluctuating for the next year and a half: "It's the volatility of a new marketplace."

Colorado, the only other state with legal marijuana sales, has a differently structured industry. Regulators have kept a lid on production, though those limits were loosened last fall as part of a planned expansion of the market.

Colorado growers still have to prove legal demand for their product, a regulatory curb aimed at preventing excess weed from spilling to other states. The result has been more demand than supply.

In Washington, many growers have unrealistic expectations about how quickly they should be able to recoup their initial investments, Simmons said. And some of the growers complaining about the low prices they're getting now also gouged the new stores amid shortages last summer.

Those include Seitz, who sold his first crop - 22 pounds - for just under $21 per gram: nearly $230,000 before his hefty $57,000 tax bill. He's about to harvest his second crop, but this time he expects to get just $4 per gram, when he has big bills to pay.

"We're running out of money," he said. "We need to make sales this month to stay operational, and we're going to be selling at losses."

Because of the high taxes on Washington's legal pot, Seitz says stores can never compete with the black market while paying growers sustainable prices.

He and other growers say it's been a mistake for the state to license so much production while the rollout of legal stores has lagged.

"If it's a natural bump from the outdoor harvest, that's one thing," said Jeremy Moberg, who is sitting on 1,500 pounds of unsold marijuana at his CannaSol Farms in north-central Washington. "If it's institutionally creating oversupply ... that's a problem."

Some retailers have been marking up the wholesale price three-fold or more - a practice that has some growers wondering if certain stores aren't cleaning up as they struggle.

"I got retailers beating me down to sell for black-market prices," said Fitz Couhig, owner of Pioneer Production and Processing in Arlington.

But two of the top-selling stores in Seattle - Uncle Ike's and Cannabis City - insist that because of their tax obligations and low demand for high-priced pot, they're not making any money either, despite each having sales of more than $600,000 per month.

Aaron Varney, a director at Dockside Cannabis, a retail shop in the Seattle suburb of Shoreline, said stores that exploit growers now could get bitten in the long run.

"Right now, the numbers will say that we're in the driver's seat," he said. "But that can change. We're looking to establish good relationships with the growers we're dealing with."

Investing In Marijuana
January 8, 2015
By Jonathan Fahey

Founders Fund, the $2 billion San Francisco venture capital firm run by Silicon Valley stars including Peter Thiel, co-founder and former CEO of Paypal, is investing in Privateer Holdings, a marijuana company that owns several pot-related brands.

The companies declined to disclose the size of the investment Thursday, but described it as a "multi-million dollar" participation in a $75 million fundraising effort by Privateer. The deal had been rumored last year.

Privateer, based in Seattle, owns the Canadian medical marijuana producer Tilray and the pot information service Leafly. It is also launching a brand of marijuana and products with the family of Bob Marley called Marley Natural.

Founders Fund partner Geoff Lewis, who is leading the firm's investment in Privateer, said in an interview that he believes the broader legalization of marijuana is inevitable.

"Public sentiment is there, and it crosses political lines," Lewis said.

There are 23 states that allow the use of marijuana for medical purposes and Colorado has legalized its recreational use.

There has been some pushback, however, despite growing public support. The states of Nebraska and Oklahoma have filed a lawsuit seeking to overturn the legalization of marijuana in Colorado, saying that they are being overrun with marijuana from across their borders.

And Founders Fund does not expect a quick turnaround on its investment in Privateer, Lewis said. Founders is investing in Privateer because it believes Privateer can eventually establish mainstream brands that will be recognized and trusted as marijuana becomes legal and socially acceptable, he said.

Privateer was founded in 2010 and has previously landed $22 million in funding.

Before the announcement Thursday, Privateer's funding came mostly through wealthy individuals and investment offices that steer private family funds.

Bud tender Maxwell Bradford shows off holiday stocking filled with more than $500 of marijuana and accessories for sale for the holiday season in a recreational marijuana shop in northwest Denver. Colorado's nascent marijuana industry is employing techniques created by traditional retailers to entice cannabis users to spend their holiday money at the dispensaries, November 20, 2014. (AP Photo/David Zalubowski)

Privateer CEO Brendan Kennedy thinks the Founders investment will lead to more professional investment into marijuana-related businesses and help advance the push toward legalization.

"One of the important milestones for this business is having access to capital, and significant capital," he said. "There will be a lot of people who wake up (now) and realize they need to look at this industry just as they have looked at other emerging industries around the world."

Founders Fund was an early investor in Facebook and has current investments in SpaceX, Spotify and Airbnb.

Jobs in Medical Marijuana
July 12, 2014
By Carla K. Johnson

The prospect of adding jobs — even as few as 30 — has led officials in many shrinking Illinois' communities to set aside any qualms about the state's legalization of medical marijuana and to get friendly with would-be growers.

The aspiring growers and their agents have been racing from town to town, shaking hands with civic leaders and promising to bring jobs and tax revenue if they're able to snag one of the 21 cultivation permits the state will grant this fall. Although not a single plant has sprouted, Illinois' new medical marijuana industry is pushing the boundaries of what is considered attractive economic development.

Michael Mayes, CEO of Chicago-based Quantum 9 Inc., a medical cannabis consulting company, poses for a photo in his Chicago office. The prospect of adding jobs, even as few as 30, has led officials in many shrinking Illinois' communities to set aside any qualms about the state's legalization of medical marijuana and to get friendly with would-be growers. Quantum 9 has helped win permits for marijuana producers in four other states, July 3, 2014. (AP Photo/Nam Y. Huh)

"It's been a long time since we've had a company say, 'Hey, we want to bring in 50 jobs and we want to bring in tax revenue to your school,'" said Liz Skinner, the mayor of Delavan, a central Illinois city of 1,700 residents. The city has annexed property optioned by Joliet-based ICC Holdings as a possible site for a marijuana cultivation center, and Skinner said a new tax increment financing district may be the next step.

Stephen Osborne, an attorney who represents a group vying for one of the growing permits, has been driving from town to town in southern Illinois and introducing himself to local officials. Mostly, he's been welcomed warmly: "It's a 'What took you so long to get here' type of response," he said. "Once you mention 30 or more jobs in a small community, they'll listen to what you have to say."

A majority of Americans — 54 percent — favor making marijuana legal at least for medicinal use, according to a Pew Research Center poll of 1,821 adults conducted in February. The survey had a margin of error of plus or minus 2.6 percentage points. New York recently became the 23rd state to make medical marijuana legal. Six months before the Illinois law was enacted, a poll by the Paul Simon Public Policy Institute at Southern Illinois University found that 63 percent of Illinoisans favored making medical use of marijuana legal.

In Illinois, city councils from Crystal Lake to Peru to Marion are considering marijuana zoning ordinances and special use permits, though the state is not tracking precisely how many. Permit seekers have simply moved on from the few communities that have voted down such proposals.

The process for building local support "starts with a conversation over the phone," explained Michael Mayes, CEO of Chicago-based Quantum 9 Inc., a cannabis consulting company that has helped win permits for marijuana producers in four other states. He said the ultimate goal would be to get a letter of recommendation from a mayor that can be submitted to the state.

Aspiring marijuana producers expect Illinois to launch a 30-day application period soon and are rushing to get their paperwork in order. To win a cultivation center permit, they'll be required to show their plans comply with local zoning rules.

Bonus points toward a winning bid can be had by submitting plans to "give back to the local community," according to draft rules under legislative review. In Delavan, Mayor Skinner said there has been talk of a cultivation center-supported gift for a drug task force, but no hard promises.

It's still unclear how many groups will compete for permits and whether applications will emerge in all regions of the state.

"What I say to others who are sniffing around, if you've not secured property, local support and a special use permit, give up now because you don't have a shot," said Tim McGraw of ICC Holdings, which plans to use the name American Cannabis Enterprises if it wins permits.

Entrepreneurs are looking for existing tax increment financing districts, according to consultants. TIF districts allow cities to finance the cost of new roads, sewers and other infrastructure through future increases in property values.

Attorney Tom Jacob and his consulting company, TIF Illinois, have worked with 65 Illinois cities on tax increment financing. Many of those cities have told him they've been approached by cannabis groups.

"It's being viewed by all our cities as a business opportunity," Jacob said. He cautions cities not to give money upfront to a developer who may not have financing. The Illinois permitting process will screen out the featherweights, he said, and towns should condition their agreements on state licensing.

"There are serious people with serious money in the state who are looking at cultivation," Jacob said. "If you have five applicants coming to your town, you want to know who the real people are with real money and interest."

Delavan's mayor said concerns about the industry evolving into recreational marijuana are fading. Recreational use remains illegal in Illinois and the conditional use permit the City Council approved specifies it's for medical cannabis only.

"Most people are very much in favor," Skinner said. "We want to make sure our town remains viable and keep our school district."

11

Avoiding the Issue for Too Long

Domestic Pot Production
January 7, 1985
By Dave Goeller

Travel guide author and marijuana legalization supporter Rick Steves holds a campaign sign in his office in Edmonds, Wash., next to a door covered with marijuana leaf-shaped notes from his staff congratulating him on the passage of a referendum legalizing marijuana in the state. In the late-1980s heyday of the "Just Say No" campaign, a man calling himself "Jerry" appeared on a Seattle radio station's midday talk show, using a pseudonym because he was a businessman, afraid of what his customers would think if they heard him criticizing U.S. marijuana laws. A quarter century later, "Jerry" had no problem using his real name - Rick Steves - as one of the main forces behind Washington's successful ballot measure to legalize, regulate and tax marijuana for adults over 21, November 26, 2012. (AP Photo/Elaine Thompson)

U.S. marijuana growers, for the first time filling more than half the nation's demand, harvested a record $16.6 billion worth of pot in 1984, according to the National Organization for the Reform of Marijuana Laws.

The estimated domestic harvest was worth 20 percent more than the 1983 crop and continued to make marijuana America's second most valuable agricultural product, NORML said in its annual cultivation report.
The U.S. Department of Agriculture estimates that the nation's corn crop last year was worth $19.5 billion, followed by hay at $11.5 billion and soybeans at $11.3 billion. Last year, the House Select Committee on Narcotics Abuse and Control estimated marijuana could be worth from $10 billion to $50 billion a year in the United States.

Illegal domestic pot farmers raised about 11 million pounds in 1984, or 55 percent of the 20-million-pound total amount available to the 30 million or more Americans using marijuana on a regular basis, according to NORML.

The group, which advocates legalization of marijuana, said that in 1983, U.S.-grown marijuana accounted for about half the pot available in this country.

The organization said it based its figures on published reports, news articles, personal interviews and law enforcement estimates and reports.

NORML said about three-quarters of the 1984 domestic crop was sinsemilla - specially cultivated seedless plants that have a higher potency and bring growers about $1,850 a pound, compared to $500 a pound for regular plants.

"The two most notable trends emerging in 1984 are an increase in indoor marijuana growing and personal-use growing," the report said. "Marijuana consumers are smoking less, consuming better quality marijuana than in the past and paying higher prices for domestically grown marijuana."

NORML said U.S. growers are benefiting from reduced pot imports, especially from Colombia, where cocaine is a more profitable drug.

The report estimated that 25 percent of all U.S. marijuana is produced indoors under plant lights by some 200,000 commercial growers and an estimated 4 million people who cultivate it for personal use in basements and closets.

"Indoor growing has become highly sophisticated and technological," said the NORML report, prepared by Joanne C. Gampel, director of the Council on Marijuana and Health.

While the number of indoor commercial growers remained stable in 1984, the personal-use growers grew by one-third last year as a response to law enforcement efforts and the rising street price of pot, according to the report.

NORML said threats by law enforcement agencies to spray outdoor crops with herbicides such as paraquat helped foster so-called personal "victory gardens" that produce from four ounces to two pounds of pot a year.

The growing trend toward indoor pot farming is making detection far more difficult for local police and federal drug agents, NORML said.

"Even though the 1984 marijuana crop was subjected to the most aggressive marijuana eradication program in United States history, the most successful states claimed that 25 percent of the marijuana plants were eradicated," the report said.

NORML said its findings "indicate the futility of marijuana enforcement. It is virtually impossible to control this market, just as it was impossible to control moonshining during alcohol Prohibition."

The West continued to be the leading marijuana growing area, producing $6.7 billion worth last year, NORML said. But the South, using sophisticated growing techniques and getting better weather, was close behind with $6.6 billion, followed by North Central states with $2.2 billion and the Northeast with $1.1 billion.

Marijuana was estimated by NORML to be the most valuable crop last year in 10 states: Alabama, California, Hawaii, Idaho, New Mexico, Oregon, South Carolina, Tennessee, Virginia and West Virginia.

NORML said the top 10 marijuana-producing states were California, $2.5 billion; Hawaii, $1 billion; Oregon, $850 million; Kentucky, $800 million; North Carolina, $650 million; Arkansas, $550 million; Oklahoma, $550 million; Tennessee, $525 million; Georgia, $500 million; and Washington, $500 million.

Marijuana Kills Herpes?
May 14, 1990
By Lee Siegel

Marijuana's active ingredient killed herpes viruses in test-tube experiments, but smoking pot won't help people with herpes and might make them prone to other diseases or cancer, a scientist said Monday, May 14, 1990.

University of South Florida microbiologist Gerald Lancz said his study may help scientists discover new anti-herpes medicines. But he warned that people with oral or genital herpes would be badly misguided if they used the findings to justify smoking marijuana, which has other harmful effects and is illegal.

"Smoking pot is not going to help your herpes, and it could make things a lot worse," said Lancz, who presented his findings Monday during the annual meeting of the American Society for Microbiology in Anaheim.

Having the drug in the bloodstream won't treat herpes sores because the concentration would be too low, Lancz said in a telephone interview.

Other studies suggest marijuana's active ingredient - delta 9 tetrahydrocanna binol, or THC - might harm the body's disease-fighting immune system, although the evidence is inconclusive, he said.

Lancz also speculated that if THC is able kill herpes viruses in people, the inactivated viruses might increase the person's vulnerability to cancer. In previous test-tube experiments, scientists have found that inactivated herpes viruses can convert healthy cells into cancer cells, he said.

"It sounds like this guy wants to show something bad (about marijuana) at all costs," said Ronald Alkana, a professor of pharmacology and toxicology at the University of Southern California.

"But he's showing it (THC) has some antiviral potential," Alkana said. "Whether or not it might help in treatment of human herpes is unknown at this time."

Alkana called the study "exciting" because it means "the THC molecule might hold a key for developing more effective treatments for herpes."

Lancz said it might be possible to find substances related to THC that don't affect the mind but do kill viruses.

Lancz and his colleagues incubated THC and various viruses in test tubes. They found that, in doses somewhat higher than found in the blood of regular marijuana users, THC killed herpes simplex virus 1, which causes the cold sores that typify oral herpes.

The scientists didn't test THC against herpes simplex 2, the genital herpes virus. But Lancz said the drug almost certainly will kill the genital herpes virus because it is so similar to the oral herpes virus.

The study found THC also killed cytomegalovirus, a herpes virus that causes flu-like symptoms in adults and is the most common infectious cause of birth defects in the United States.

Richard "Cheech" Marin, left, and Thomas Chong are shown at a party at the Friars Club for their new movie, "Cheech and Chong's Nice Dreams," in New York City. Those rumors about an on-screen reunion of Cheech Marin and Tommy Chong? Reefer madness, Marin says. The 59-year-old actor, half of the Cheech & Chong comedy duo that embodied 1970s and 1980s marijuana humor, said there will be no future joint efforts with Chong, June 4, 1981. (AP Photo/Nancy Kaye)

But "even if smoking marijuana helped control herpes, the costs of marijuana smoking - getting busted and losing your job, for one thing - certainly overshadow any of the potential benefits of treating herpes," said Ronald K. Siegel, a psychopharmacologist at the University of California, Los Angeles.

He added that marijuana causes lung problems and there's good evidence it causes changes in hormones and behavior, including reducing motivation.

In another test-tube study, scheduled for presentation at the microbiology meeting on Tuesday, University of South Florida microbiology student Kirk Trisler found THC suppressed the normal growth of disease-fighting white blood cells and disrupted their ability to kill tumor cells.

A number of previous studies have shown THC can impair the performance of various components of the human immune system, while others have found no such damage. Siegel, Alkana and Lancz agreed there is no evidence demonstrating that pot smokers are more prone to diseases, except for bronchitis and other smoke-related lung problems.

One Step Forward, Two Steps Back
November 7, 1990
By Brian S. Akre

Alaskans have voted to again make private possession of marijuana a crime, striking down the nation's most liberal pot law.

Fifty-five percent of voters approved the measure.

For 15 years, Alaska law has permitted adults to possess less than 4 ounces of the drug in their homes and other private places.

Ballot Measure 2 will make possession of small amounts of marijuana a misdemeanor punishable by up to 90 days in jail and a $1,000 fine. The new law takes effect in late February.

"It's wonderful," said Marie Majewske, the Anchorage grandmother who led the initiative campaign. "I have great faith in the people of this state. I truly believed they would do the right thing.

"I think that this will say to people that the law didn't work, and we need to be looking in the other direction, toward a drug-free environment for our children. The only way to do that is to tell them it's illegal."

The race was closer than most observers expected. Polls had shown the measure supported by a nearly 2-to-1 margin as late as a week ago.

"It certainly doesn't look like a mandate, does it?" said Glenda Straube, campaign manager for Alaskans for Privacy, which led opposition to the measure.

Straube said the measure will be challenged in court based on the strong privacy clause in the Alaska Constitution.

"We've had people around the state call and volunteer to be arrested" for a test case, she said.

Legal Marijuana to Fight AIDS
November 21, 1990
By Pete Yost

Prepared marijuana is displayed for sale for those who posses a medical marijuana card, inside a dispensary in the small Rocky Mountain town of Nederland, Colo. Since the 1970 founding of the National Organization for the Reform of Marijuana Laws, reform efforts had centered on the unfairness of laws to the recreational user. That began to change as doctors noticed marijuana's ability to relieve pain, quell nausea and improve the appetites of cancer and AIDS patients. The conversation shifted in the 1990s toward medical marijuana laws. On Nov. 6, 2012, Colorado and Washington state legalized its recreational use, November 19, 2012. (AP Photo/Brennan Linsley)

An AIDS patient received a government-approved shipment of marijuana Wednesday to help ease the pain of his disease, a private group said.

"I have a lot to be thankful for this Thanksgiving," the 34-year-old Virginia man said in a statement released by the Alliance for Cannabis Therapeutics, which helped him present his case.

The man, identified by ACT only as "Danny," is the second AIDS patient in the United States to receive marijuana approved by the Food and Drug Administration.

An FDA spokeswoman confirmed the agency gave approval Tuesday for someone to use marijuana. ACT quoted Danny as saying the drug "helps me cope with this terrible disease."

Marijuana reduced the patient's nausea, vomiting and weight-loss caused by the AIDS virus and restored his appetite, said the group, which favors making marijuana available legally for medical uses.

The FDA has allowed marijuana use by patients for compassionate purposes in at least two dozen instances since 1976.

ACT's president, Robert Randall, a glaucoma patient, was the first to win FDA approval.

"Marijuana's use is widespread and rapidly growing among AIDS patients," and Danny's case will encourage them to demand an end to its ban in medicine, Randall said.

Marijuana is classified as a Schedule I drug by the Drug Enforcement Administration, making it available only for research. DEA administrators for more than 14 years have rejected bids to make marijuana available to medical patients.

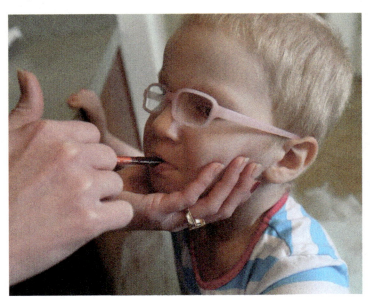

Three year old severe cancer patient Dahlia Barnhart gets cannabis treatment from her mother Moriah with an oral syringe, at her home in Colorado Springs. Colo., A panel of legislative leaders on Wednesday, Oct. 15, 2014 approved a bill on a 13-5 vote that would limit how many plants marijuana caregivers can grow for their patients, April 29, 2014. (AP Photo/Brennan Linsley)

In 1988, an administrative law judge recommended that DEA make marijuana available by prescription for the treatment of life- and sense-threatening diseases. The DEA administrator rejected the recommendation.

Advocates are appealing that decision to the U.S. Court of Appeals in Washington, D.C.

The government-supplied drug, in cigarette form, came from a pharmacy in northern Virginia, ACT said.

Across the Pacific
January 22, 2015
By Rod McGuirk

The case of an Australian father who is facing prison for allegedly giving his cancer-stricken 2-year-old daughter cannabis to relieve her pain has triggered a groundswell of momentum for a campaign to legalize marijuana for medical purposes in the country.

The 30-year-old father, who cannot be named under Australian law, was arrested outside his daughter's hospital in Brisbane on Jan. 2 for allegedly putting cannabis oil in her food. He was charged with supplying a dangerous drug to a minor and faces up to 25 years in prison if convicted.

An online petition calling on the Queensland state Premier Campbell Newman to intervene on the father's behalf had more than 155,000 supporters on Thursday.

Sen. Richard Di Natale, health spokesman for the minor Greens Party, a leading advocate for legal medical marijuana and a former doctor, said the case is helping turn Australians against a blanket ban on marijuana.

"I've been surprised that the issue (medical marijuana) within the Australian community is as big an issue as it clearly is," Di Natale said Thursday.

At the father's first court appearance, a magistrate released him on bail but barred him from any contact with his daughter, who was recently diagnosed with advanced neuroblastoma, a type of cancer that is almost exclusive to babies and children.

The court relaxed the father's bail conditions last week, allowing him to visit his daughter in the hospital under medical supervision. He is to return to court on Feb. 23. He has yet to enter a plea.

A small crowd of medical cannabis advocates held a rally outside last week's court session. A small group of mothers of terminally ill children held a similar demonstration this week outside the state health department.

"As a mom, all I want is quality of life for my child because the drugs have just done nothing for him," said demonstrator Rozanne Burley, whose teenage son has a form of intractable epilepsy called Dravet's syndrome.

Premier Newman, a conservative, has said he is sympathetic to the idea of medicinal marijuana, but any decision should be based on information from federal health authorities. Medical authorities have questioned the medicinal benefits.

The conservative government of Australia's most populous state, New South Wales, announced last month that medicinal cannabis will be trialed in treating children with severe epilepsy, terminally ill adults and patients who suffer nausea and vomiting as a result of chemotherapy.

The center-left government of the next most populous state, Victoria, also announced in December it hopes to become the first state in Australia to legalize medical marijuana by the end of 2015. No Australian state leader has opposed such a move.

Prime Minister Tony Abbott, a conservative, has opened the door to a federal law allowing cannabis to be used for medical purposes throughout Australia.

"I have no problem with the medical use of cannabis, just as I have no problem with the medical use of opiates," Abbott wrote in a letter to Sydney broadcaster and influential conservative commentator Alan Jones last August.

Di Natale introduced legislation in Parliament in November that would create an independent regulator responsible for licensing the growing, manufacture and distribution of medicinal cannabis. Individual states could opt out of any form of legal marijuana.

While legislation proposed by a party outside government usually fails in Australia's political system, Di Natale's bill has the backing of the multiparty Parliamentary Group for Drug Policy and Law Reform.

Di Natale said the medical marijuana cause has gained momentum because of an extraordinary consensus among political leaders on the issue, with conservative support particularly critical.

"It has happened quickly, but it's happened because there has been a little bit of leadership shown," Di Natale said.

The charged father did not immediately reply to an emailed request for comment Thursday the 22nd of January.

Medical marijuana dispensary proprietor Dawn Darington demonstrates to clients how to use a marijuana product tincture in Seattle. Darington has seen patients wracked by AIDS and cancer. She's also seen "patients" who show up for a free pot brownie and never come back. Now, Washington is pushing forward with plans to entice the latter into its new world of legal, taxed recreational pot, and advocates like Darington say they're worried about where that's going to leave those who actually need cannabis, October 18, 2013. (AP Photo/Elaine Thompson)

Colorado Reviews Marijuana Health
February 2, 2015
By Kristen Wyatt

Colorado released a sweeping report Monday about marijuana and health - everything from pot's effect on drivers, asthma, cancer rates and birth defects.

The 188-page report doesn't include new research on marijuana. Instead, it's a review of what its authors call limited existing studies.

The report looks at studies showing that risk of a motor vehicle crash doubles among drivers with recent marijuana use, and that heavy use of marijuana is associated with impaired memory.

Other highlights from the report:

- In adults, heavy use of marijuana is associated with impaired memory, persisting a week or more after quitting.

- Maternal use of marijuana during pregnancy is associated with negative effects on exposed offspring, including decreased academic ability, cognitive function and attention.

- Regular marijuana use by adolescents and young adults is strongly associated with developing psychotic symptoms and disorders such as schizophrenia in adulthood.

The Colorado Department of Public Health and Environment review was ordered by state lawmakers. A panel of doctors met for several months to compile the survey, which was delivered to lawmakers last week.

The report also lays out areas where there is limited evidence, or where research is lacking.

For example, the report found insufficient evidence to say how long after smoking pot a person is impaired. Other areas of scanty research:

- Doctors noted there is little available research on the health effects of edible or concentrated marijuana.

- Marijuana smoke contains "many of the same cancer-causing chemicals as tobacco smoke." But doctors noted there is "limited" or "mixed" evidence to suggest pot-smoking is associated with greater risk of lung cancer or other respiratory health effects.

The doctors suggested additional education about the health effects of marijuana and asked for increased public-health surveys about how people use pot.

Researchers noted that because marijuana use was illegal nationwide until 1996 - when California voters approved the first medical uses for pot - research is extremely limited. Marijuana research has historically looked for adverse effects, not possible health benefits.

"This legal fact introduces both funding bias and publication bias into the body of literature related to marijuana use," authors noted.

Colorado last year funded eight studies to examine possible health benefits of marijuana, including treatment for seizures, Parkinson's disease and post-traumatic stress disorder. Those studies, totaling about $8 million, may not have results for several years.

Pot for Kids in the Marijuana Nation
January 26, 2015
By Lindsey Tanner

This file photo shows parents of children who suffer from epilepsy. With virtually no hard proof that medical marijuana benefits sick children, and evidence that it may harm developing brains, the drug should only be used for severely ill kids who have no other treatment option, the nation's most influential pediatricians group says in a new policy, January 13, 2015. (AP Photo/David Goldman, File)

With virtually no hard proof that medical marijuana benefits sick children, and evidence that it may harm developing brains, the drug should only be used for severely ill kids who have no other treatment option, the nation's most influential pediatricians group says in a new policy.

Some parents insist that medical marijuana has cured their kids' troublesome seizures or led to other improvements, but the American Academy of Pediatrics' new policy says rigorous research is needed to verify those claims.

To make it easier to study and develop marijuana-based treatments, the group recommends removing marijuana from the government's most restrictive drug category, which includes heroin, LSD and other narcotics with no accepted medical use, and switching it to the category which includes methadone and oxycodone.

The recommended switch "could help make a big difference in promoting more research," said Dr. Seth Ammerman, the policy's lead author and a professor of pediatrics and adolescent medicine at Stanford University.

The academy's qualified support may lead more pediatricians to prescribe medical marijuana, but the group says pediatric use should only be considered "for children with life-limiting or severely debilitating conditions and for whom current therapies are inadequate."

The academy also repeated its previous advice against legalizing marijuana for recreational use by adults, suggesting that may enable easier access for kids. It does not address medical marijuana use in adults.

Utah's Gov. Gary Herbert, center, looks on during the H.B.105 bill signing ceremony at the state Capitol, in Salt Lake City. Utah will begin issuing registration cards Tuesday, July 8, 2014, for its limited medical marijuana program targeting adults and children with severe epilepsy, March 25, 2014. (AP Photo/Rick Bowmer, File)

Studies have linked recreational marijuana use in kids with ill effects on health and brain development, including problems with memory, concentration, attention, judgment and reaction time, the group's policy emphasizes.

The policy was published online Monday in Pediatrics. It updates and expands the group's 2004 policy.

Since then, the marijuana movement has grown substantially. Recreational and medical marijuana use is legal for adults in four states - Alaska, Colorado, Oregon and Washington. Nineteen other states and Washington D.C., have laws allowing medical marijuana use only and most allow children to qualify, according to Morgan Fox of the Marijuana Policy Project, a national group that advocates marijuana policy reform and tracks state laws.
"The cart is so far ahead of the horse related to this drug," said Dr. Angus Wilfong, of Texas Children's Hospital in Houston. Marijuana has dozens of chemical components that need to be studied just like any drug to determine safety, proper doses and potential side effects, he said.

Wilfong was involved in a recently completed international study involving 30 children with severe epilepsy. About half got an experimental drug made with a marijuana compound that doesn't make users high; the others received dummy medicine. Study results are being analyzed. Wilfong said five children from his hospital were involved and while he doesn't know if any of them got the marijuana drug, none suffered any serious side effects.

Wilfong said he has a young seizure patient in a different, less rigorous study who has shown dramatic improvement after several months on the marijuana-based treatment, "but that doesn't prove it was due to the" experimental drug," he said.

Marijuana Visualized

1995

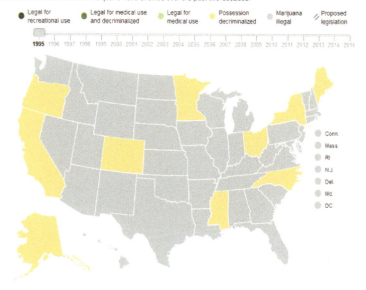

2005

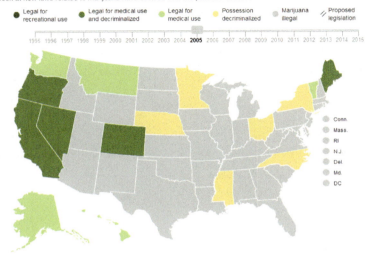

2015

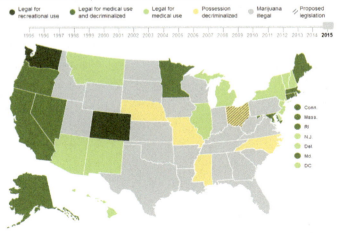

Percentage of Americans who support or oppose legal marijuana:

● Support ● Oppose

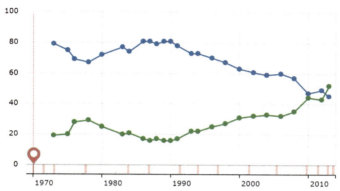

SOURCES: General Social Survey, AP-NORC Center for Public Affairs Research

Percentage of Americans who support legal marijuana, by party:

● Democrat ● Independent ● Republican

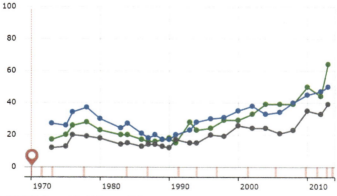

SOURCES: General Social Survey, AP-NORC Center for Public Affairs Research

Percentage of Americans who support legal marijuana, by education:

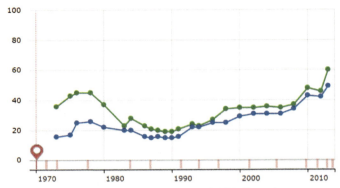

SOURCES: General Social Survey, AP-NORC Center for Public Affairs Research

Percentage of Americans who support legal marijuana, by generation:

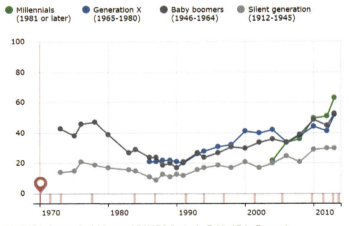

SOURCES: General Social Survey, AP-NORC Center for Public Affairs Research

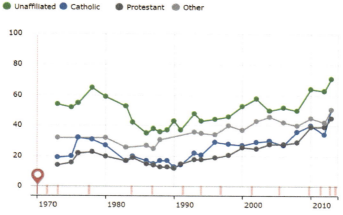

Percentage of Americans who support legal marijuana, by religion:
● Unaffiliated ● Catholic ● Protestant ● Other

SOURCES: General Social Survey, AP-NORC Center for Public Affairs Research

THE AP EMERGENCY RELIEF FUND

When Hurricane Katrina hit the Gulf Coast in 2005, many Associated Press staffers and their families were personally affected. AP employees rallied to help these colleagues by setting up the AP Emergency Relief Fund, which has since become a source of crucial assistance worldwide to AP staff and their families who have suffered damage or loss as a result of conflict or natural disasters.

Established as an independent 501(c)(3), the Fund provides a quick infusion of cash to help staff and their families rebuild homes, relocate and repair and replace damaged possessions.

The AP donates the net proceeds from AP Essentials, AP's company store, to the Fund.

HOW TO GIVE

In order to be ready to help the moment emergencies strike, the Fund relies on the generous and ongoing support of the extended AP community. Donations can be made any time at http://www.ap.org/relieffund and are tax deductible.

On behalf of the AP staffers and families who receive aid in times of crisis, the AP Emergency Relief Fund Directors and Officers thank you.

ALSO AVAILABLE FROM AP EDITIONS

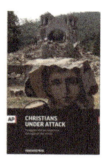

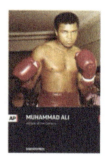

CPSIA information can be obtained at www.ICGtesting.com
Printed in the USA
LVOW05s1933280415

436412LV00041B/263/P

9 781633 530362